Carbon Shinai
カーボンシナイ

- CF-Type
- DB-Type
- K1-Type
- K2-Type

Orange · Red · Yellow

We have improved the official Carbon Shinai rubber stopper.
The NEW official rubber stopper.
￥300 (domestic Japanese price)

WARNING!!
When using your Carbon Shinai..... Never use anything other than our official rubber stopper on your Carbon Shinai !!

1. To prevent injury, please use our official rubber stopper. Do not use stoppers made for conventional bamboo shinai on your Carbon Shinai, as there is a risk of injury to your opponent if the tip breaks through and enters their men grill.
2. When choosing a sakigawa (leather tip), make sure that it is more than 5cm in length and completely covers our rubber stopper. If the sakigawa is shorter than 5cm, there is a risk of injury to your opponent if a slat slips out and enters their men grill.
3. Do not shave the plastic surface of your Carbon Shinai. If you shave the surface, the black carbon fiber will be exposed, causing damage that may result in injury to your opponent.
4. Always check the condition of the surface of your Carbon Shinai before and during use. As soon as you notice any cracks, or peeling of the surface, or if black carbon fiber is exposed on any part of the outside, inside or edges of the Shinai, or you notice any other damage, stop using the shinai immediately. There is a danger of injury to your opponent if your Carbon Shinai is split or broken.
5. When tying the nakayui (leather binding), either tie a knot in the tsuru-ito (cord), or tie one end of the nakayui to the tsuru-ito, or by another means ensuring that is does not move up and down during use. If there is any damage whatsoever to the sakigawa, tsukagawa (hilt), rubber stopper, tsuru-ito and so on, replace them immediately.
6. If the tip of the Carbon Shinai is damaged, or a slat is protuding out of the sakigawa, there is a danger that it could enter your opponent's men grill and injure them.

Kendogu Revolution

Mu-Jun Men
武楯面

WARNING!!
1. Under no circumstances should organic solvents (such as thinner, alcohol, benzene, toluene, acetone, gasoline, kerosene, etc.), acidic or alkali chemicals, domestic cleansers, car cleansers, or anti-mist sprays, be used to clean the shield. These substances will cause the shield to deteriorate, leading to clouding, cracking or breaking, thereby resulting in danger of injury to the face.
2. Should the shield develop deep scratches or cracks on either the outer or inner surface, discontinue use of the shield immediately, and replace it with an undamaged shield. If the shield is used in such a condition, there is a danger of it breaking, causing injury to the face.
3. It should be fully understood that, as with the traditional Japanese Kendo-Men (mask), there is still the danger of injury to the face through fragments of broken bamboo or Carbon Shinai pieces penetrating through areas not covered by the shield.

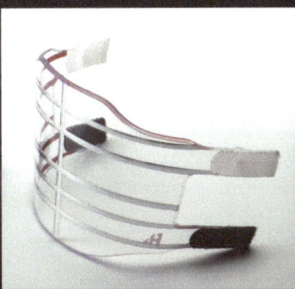

SG-Type

- SCIENCE TO SEEK SAFETY -
HASEGAWA
HASEGAWA CORPORATION

WEB : http://kendo.hasegawakagaku.co.jp/
Email : contact@hasegawakagaku.co.jp

Carbon Shinai — Points to be checked

DANGER !!   **ATTENTION !!**

Before these happen.....

Although the Carbon Shinai is much more durable than a conventional bamboo one, it will inevitably become damaged since it is a sword that is used to repeatedly strike and thrust your opponent. Therefore, inspect the condition of the surface, sides or reverse of the Carbon Shinai's slats before, during and after use, and stop using it immediately should damage like in the following pictures be observed. (These pictures are just a few examples of many.)

- Damage on the surface

- An unglued surface sheet

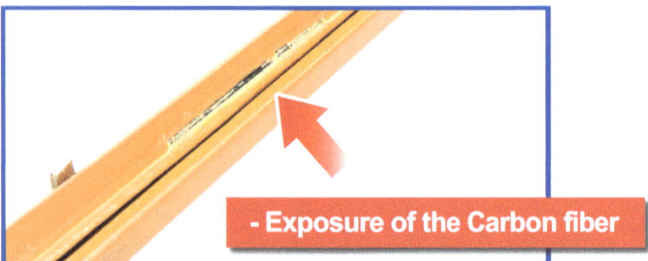

- Exposure of the Carbon fiber

- Longitudinal crack on the surface

- Damage and ungluing of the surface

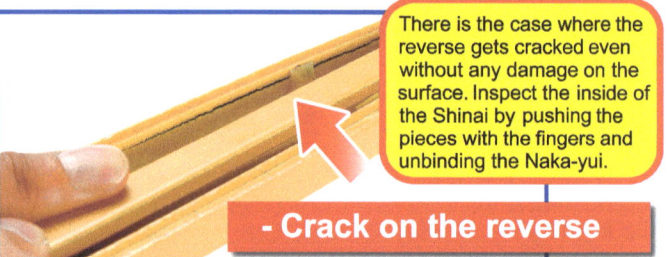

- Crack on the reverse

There is the case where the reverse gets cracked even without any damage on the surface. Inspect the inside of the Shinai by pushing the pieces with the fingers and unbinding the Naka-yui.

HASEGAWA-KOTE

- Detachable and washable "Tenouchi" is easy to wash and dry.

- "Tenouchi" is replaceable when torn. No need to repair.

Kote (Main part)

Tenouchi (Inner)

- SCIENCE TO SEEK SAFETY -

HASEGAWA CORPORATION
http://kendo.hasegawakagaku.co.jp/

KENDO WORLD Volume 8.1 December 2015 Contents

Editorial From Shinai to Lightsaber — 2

The 63rd All Japan Kendo Championships — 6

The 63rd All Japan Kendo Championships in Numbers — 12

Inishie wo Kangaeru — 15

Takano Sasaburō's *Kendo* — 16

sWords of Wisdom
"Chikushōshin wo sare" — 22

Kendo for Adults — 24

Reidan-jichi Part 20 **Waza Basics: Debana Waza** — 31

Kendo or: How I Learned to Stop Worrying and Love the Olympics — 32

Kendo From Basics — 38

Bujutsu Jargon Part 8 — 46

Book Review
The Book of Samurai — 48

Budo Finder Interview — 50

Belabouring Each Other Fiendishly — 52

Dojo File
Wakakoma Kenshikai — 59

Movement and Stillness
Meiji Shrine Kobudō Demonstrations — 62

Book Review
Helmets and Stirrups — 69

Samurai Skills: Part 1 — 72

Hagakure and the Spirit of Zanshin — 74

"On Location"
The Continuing Story of Kendo Wa — 76

The Shugyō Mind: Part 1 — 79

Shinai Sagas
A Lonely Stone — 81

Dojo File
The Vietnam Kendo Clubs Association — 84

Musō Jikiden Eishin-ryū Riai
The Meaning of the Kata: Part 3 — 86

Uncle Kotay's Kendo Korner
Part 1: sonkyo in kendo — 96

Kendo World Staff
- Bunkasha International President & Editor-in-Chief— Alex Bennett PhD
- Bunkasha International Vice President & Assistant Editor—Michael Ishimatsu-Prime MA
- Bunkasha International Vice President & Graphic Design—Shishikura 'Kan' Masashi
- Bunkasha International Vice President—Hamish Robison
- Bunkasha International Vice President—Michael Komoto MA
- Bunkasha International General Manager—Baptiste Tavernier MA
- Senior Consultants—Yonemoto Masayuki, Shima Masahiko

KW Staff Writers | Translators | Photographers | Graphic Designer | Sub-editors

- Axel Pilgrim PhD
- Blake Bennett PhD
- Bruce Flanagan MA
- Bryan Peterson
- Charlie Kondek
- Gabriel Weitzner
- Honda Sōtarō PhD
- Imafuji Masahiro MBA
- Jeff Broderick
- Kate Sylvester PhD
- Sergio Boffa PhD
- Stephen Nagy PhD
- Steven Harwood MA
- Stuart Gibson
- Taylor Winter
- Tony Cundy
- Trevor Jones
- Tyler Rothmar
- Yamaguchi Remi
- Vivian Yung
- Yulin Zhuang

KW would like to thank the following people and organisations for their valuable cooperation:
- All Japan Kendo Federation
- Hasegawa Teiichi - President, Hasegawa Corporation
- *Kendo Jidai* Magazine
- *Kendo Nihon* Magazine
- Nippon Budokan Foundation
- Nine Circles
- Shogun Kendogu
- TOZANDO

Guest Writers
- Antony Cummins (Historical Ninjutsu Research Team)
- Hatano Toshio (Kendo Kyōshi 8-dan)
- Hirakawa Nobuo (Kendo Kyōshi 8-dan)
- Kim Taylor (Iaido 7-dan, sdksupplies.com)
- Maxime Chouinard (hemamisfits.com)
- Ōya Minoru (Prof. International Budo University; Kendo Kyōshi 7-dan)
- Serge Hendrickx (Wakakoma Kendo Club)
- Tran Thanh Tung (Vietnam Kendo Clubs Association)

COPYRIGHT 2016 Bunkasha International Corporation. No part of this publication may be reproduced in any form whatsoever without written permission from the publisher, except by writers who are permitted to quote brief passages for the purpose of review or reference. Kindly contact Bunkasha International Corporation at info@kendo-world.com.

Editorial Conventions Used in KW Inevitably in a magazine of this nature, many non-English words appear in the text. All Japanese words are italicised and include macrons (ū, ō) etc., apart from common place names and nouns, and words in some captions and headings. As a general exception, KW treats all the martial arts (budo), such as kendo, iaido, jodo, ranks, and so on as Anglicised words without using macrons. Japanese names are written in accordance to the traditional Japanese manner of family name followed by given name. Traditional *ryūha* are written with capitals and therefore are not italicised. 'Kata' with a capital 'K' refers to the set of Nippon Kendo Kata, and *kata* refers to set forms in general. The masculine personal pronoun is used throughout the text in some articles in the interest of readability, and is in no way meant to slight the significant contributions made by female kendoka.

Editorial
From Shinai to Lightsaber

By Michael Ishimatsu-Prime
Photos: Courtesy of ESPN

Alex has retired to the mountains of Middle Earth—a.k.a. New Zealand—for some much needed R&R, so I've assumed responsibility for the next three pages.

2015 was a big year for kendo and *Kendo World*. In May, the Nippon Budokan in Tokyo hosted the 16th World Kendo Championships, and greeted delegations from 56 countries and regions for the biggest event to date. All the members of the *Kendo World* team were involved in the WKC in some capacity, either as a competitor, manager, coach, interpreter, official, shop staff, cameraman or reporter.

According to the All Japan Kendo Federation's "Purpose of Practising Kendo", one of kendo's aims is "…to promote peace and prosperity among all peoples." In the same vein, the Budō Charter's "Philosophy of Budō", formulated by the Japanese Budo Association in 2008, states: "The Budō arts serve as a path to self-perfection. This elevation of the human spirit will contribute to social prosperity and harmony, and ultimately, benefit the people of the world." While these are lofty ideals, an event such as the WKC does contribute to this in some way. The championships did not solve any of the world's conflicts, which have only intensified throughout the year, but it did bring together people from many different places and backgrounds throughout the world—people who under normal circumstances might not meet or mix. If not creating peace, it likely strengthened friendships and created new ones, which cannot be a bad thing.

No discussion of 2015 would be complete without mentioning *Star Wars Episode VII: The Force Awakens*. I haven't looked forward to a film as much as this since *Star Wars Episode I: The Phantom Menace*, and we all know how that turned out. I therefore tried to rein in my expectations for this latest instalment, but failed miserably and got hopelessly caught up in all the hype. Like in 1999, it was a chance to feel like a kid again. This time, however, I was a father and was able to get my two boys involved and share a big part of my childhood with them, despite them only being two years old and four months.

Ray Park

But how does *The Force Awakens* relate to kendo, and why should it be mentioned in this magazine? Well, in the run-up to its release on December 18, ESPN, an American TV sports network, broadcast a documentary titled *Evolution of the Lightsaber Duel* in which kendo was central as it was used as the base for the exciting face-offs.

In *Evolution of the Lightsaber Duel*, giving the viewer some historical background to kendo were K7-dan Ōya Minoru, International Budo University professor and *Kendo World* contributor, and K8-dan Terachi Kenjirō of the Tokyo Metropolitan Police. Also featured were Chris Yang, Brandon Harada, and Shuntaro Shinada of Team U.S.A.; the film's stunt coordinators; and interviews with some of the *Star Wars* cast, past and present. There was also a lot of footage showing Team U.S.A. training for the WKC, and highlights of the semi-final and final matches of the men's team competition.

George Lucas was heavily inspired by the samurai movies of Akira Kurosawa, something that is evident in the original trilogy. Indeed, the characters of R2-D2 and C-3PO are influenced by those of Tahei and Matashichi from *Hidden Fortress* (1958); Darth Vader's costume is reminiscent of samurai armour, particularly the helmet; and of course, the Jedi use swords. And as for the word "Jedi", it is believed that George Lucas took that from the Japanese word "*jidai-geki*", meaning "period drama", but which more usually refers to samurai-era novels and films. More important for us, however, was that at several points in the documentary, kendo was discussed as being the base for a lot of the lightsaber duels, and Mark Hamill actually commented that he received training in kendo in preparation for his scenes.

Kendo's influence is clear to see. For example, in *Episode IV* when Obi-Wan Kenobi fights Darth Vader, both start in a position very similar to *chūdan-no-kamae*. Their *kensen* are a little too high for my liking, but perhaps they are using a version that is only taught once you reach the level of Jedi. Also, towards the end of that fight when they both are framed by the hangar doorway, it is possible to

Editorial

see Vader using *okuri-ashi* to advance towards Obi-Wan, albeit with the left foot forward—there's nothing in the rules wrong with that! When Vader realises that his *seme* is ineffective against his former master's *kamae* and cannot create the opening needed to execute a successful strike, he again uses *okuri-ashi* to retreat and regroup.

In *The Empire Strikes Back* when Darth Vader and Luke Skywalker fight in Bespin, Vader begins the encounter employing *katate-waza*. In fact, it's more like a fencing stance as he is holding his left hand out. Realising that Luke is stronger than he originally thought, he reverts to his two-handed *morote* grip, à la kendo. Towards the end of that fight, just before Vader unleashes genealogical terror upon Luke, he uses *maki-waza* to flick Luke's lightsaber away from his centre to expose his *kote*. Oh boy does Vader have a mean *kote*.

In *Attack of the Clones*, for a short while both Count Dooku and Anakin Skywalker employ *jōdan-no-kamae*, before Anakin loses the encounter, again by a mean *kote*. Dooku's *kote* is off target but effective nonetheless. The Sith might have questionable morals, but they do have strong *kote-waza*.

The Phantom Menace actually has my favourite lightsaber duel in all of the much-maligned prequels, that being the one between Obi-Wan and Darth Maul. Maul starts the encounter using the double-ended lightsaber, but when Obi-Wan cuts it in half, Maul then employs the standard two-handed kendo grip used in the rest of the films. In the *Evolution of the Lightsaber Duel* documentary, Ray Park, the actor who plays Maul, says that as he is a Wushu practitioner he would have used the sword one-handed at that moment. Being an accomplished martial artist himself, it is possible that he could have suggested using the lightsaber in the way in which he is familiar, but ultimately the decision was made to go two-handed.

I could go on and on about the lightsaber duels in all of the *Star Wars* films, but I'll just finish by saying that in my opinion, the final fight between Luke and Vader in *Return of the Jedi* is the best. None of the other fights come as close to that one in terms of emotion, and many of the fights in the prequels end up being tedious in comparison.

As a group, I think that us kendoka are quite precious about what we do, and do not like it when kendo is misrepresented. While there were a couple of moments in *Evolution of the Lightsaber Duel* that made me wince a little (Mark Hamill leaning on his *shinai*, but he's Luke Skywalker so gets a pass), I thought that on the whole this documentary was a great introduction to kendo if people had not seen it before. More than that, however, was the fact that kendo was on primetime TV.

People on Facebook have already commented on how numbers for beginner classes have increased, most likely as a result of seeing *Evolution of the Lightsaber Duel*. Some have commented that many of these new recruits won't stick with kendo when they realise that it's actually not like a lot of the duels seen in the *Star Wars* films, but some will. And whatever gets people interested is a good thing. For me it was seeing kendo in *Black Rain* starring Michael Douglas and Takakura Ken, although my first lesson was about 15 years after that.

For *Kendo World*, 2015 was a big year, too. We've started to release *Kendo World* in the Zinio ebook format. This has proved to be very popular, and if you're reading this editorial on a PC, iPhone or Android device, thank you for making the switch. If you're reading the paper version, thank you for your custom, but please check the Zinio edition out. We've also re-released *Kendo World* Vol.1 and Vol.2 on Zinio format, which have also been very popular. Looking back at those issues, it's amazing how far we've come in the 15 years we've been publishing *Kendo World*. Back then we had no idea how to make a magazine, but with guts and determination we soldiered on.

It's looking like 2016 will be a big year for *Kendo World*, too. We're hoping to release volumes three, four, five, and six on the Zinio platform so that our entire catalogue will be available and ready to read on a mobile or tablet. Imagine that, the entire catalogue of *Kendo World* always on your person! It could be read on the way to the dojo, in the dojo, on the way home from the dojo, or in the pub while on the way home from the dojo!

We also have several books on the slate for 2016, but perhaps the biggest will be an English translation of K8-Dan Hirakawa Nobuo-sensei's *Kendo From Basics*. As a taster, a short section of that book appears in this edition. When completed, this will be the most comprehensive book on kendo's techniques available in English.

Thank you for your support through 2015, and we hope that you have a great budo year in 2016!

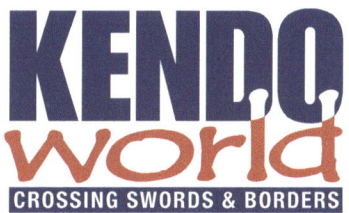

PUBLICATIONS

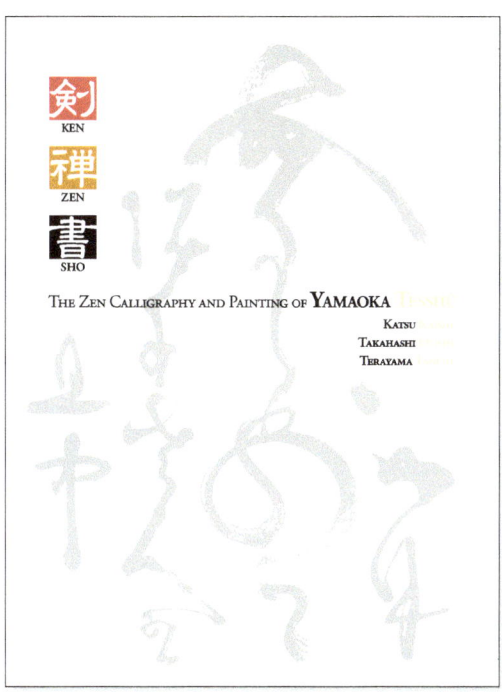

Ken Zen Sho
The Zen Calligraphy and Painting of Yamaoka Tesshu

Yamaoka Tesshu (1836-1888) was a Japanese master of the sword, Zen and calligraphy. This full-colour book on the Zen art of Yamaoka Tesshu features reproductions of extremely valuable calligraphy pieces, and also a number of essays about the relationship between swordsmanship, the study of Zen, and calligraphy. Each one of the works presented are translated into English, and its significance explained in detailed captions. Some fantastic specimens of Zen calligraphy by Tesshu's famous contemporaries Katsu Kaishu and Takahashi Deishu (Tesshu's brother-in-law), and modern master Terayama Tanchu are also featured.

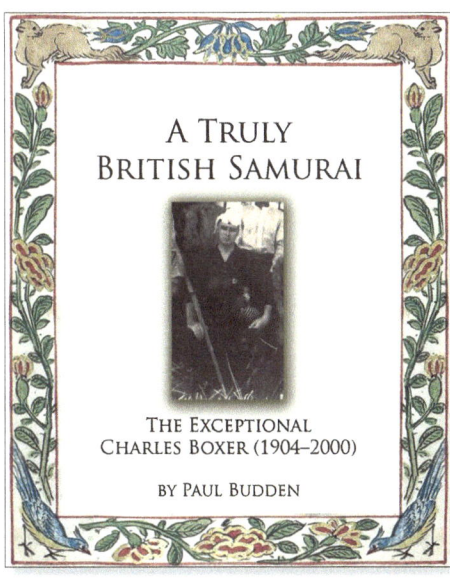

A Truly British Samurai
The Exceptional Charles Boxer

Budo Perspectives

Kendo:
Approaches for all Levels

More info → www.kendo-world.com

THE 63RD ALL JAPAN KENDO CHAMPIONSHIPS

By Michael Ishimatsu-Prime

The subtitle of my analysis of the 62nd All Japan Kendo Championships (AJKC) in *Kendo World* 7.4 was the following question: A Changing of the Guard? This was in reference to the youthfulness of that AJKC, and how the older, more established competitors did not really shine. That tournament will be remembered for the AJKC's youngest ever winner: Takenouchi Yūya, a third-year student at the University of Tsukuba who was aged 21 years and 5 months.

Students have been making great inroads in the AJKC in recent years, most notably Hatakenaka Kōsuke and Andō Shō, who were both Kokushikan University students when they first qualified, and who now represent the police forces of Tokyo and Hokkaido respectively. And of course there is Takenouchi, the most successful of them all. Takenouchi qualified again this year as a Fukuoka representative. In addition to Takenouchi, there were two more students that qualified, and they are getting younger! Before Takenouchi's victory in 2014, the youngest ever champion was company worker Kuwahara Tetsuaki, who took the title at the 8th AJKC in 1960. However, with the other two students that qualified this year, there was a chance that we would not have to wait another 54 years to see the next youngest-ever champion. One was Umegatani Kakeru, a 20-year-old second-year student from Chuo University. Despite his young age, he has already been a very successful competitor, placing second in the National Sports Meet and third in the University Student Team Championships. What is most impressive, however, is that he has won and finished second in the University Student Individual Championships in two entries, and his victory was when he was a first-year. At the University Student Individual Championships in July 2015, Umegatani faced Takenouchi (defending AJKC champion) in the semifinal and defeated him with a *men* strike right at the beginning of *enchō*. Just a month later, though, Takenouchi got revenge and beat Umegatani in the semi-final of the Fukuoka qualifying tournament for the AJKC, which meant that Umegatani had to win the third-place playoff against the policeman, Ogura Yūtarō, which he did. Interestingly, not one of Fukuoka's three

representatives were police: two students and a company worker made up their ranks.

Representing Tottori, the other student to qualify was Sanada Hiroyuki (20), a second-year student from the National Institute of Fitness and Sports Kanoya in Kagoshima. Like Umegatani, Sanada already has an impressive competition record winning the University Student Team Championships, the Inter-High Team Competition, the High School Senbatsu team competition, and was runner-up in the individual division of the latter.

Usually competitors in the AJKC are 5-dan and above, although recently there has been an increase in the number of 4-dan. It is very rare to see a 3-dan competitor, but that's the grade that both Umegatani and Sanada held. They were unable to take the 4-dan grading because of their age. There was another 3-dan who also qualified this year: Jinbo Shōta, 23, a policeman from Niigata who joined the police straight from high school.

This year there were two 7-dan kenshi in the mix: the evergreen Yoneya Yūichi (39, Saitama) and Gonpei Noriyasu (38, Tokyo). This was Yoneya's twelfth entry and Gonpei's third.

Still the most successful competitor around today is Tokyo's R6-dan Uchimura Ryōichi (35), who was making his tenth appearance. He has won the AJKC three times, been runner-up three times, and third once, and with the exception of the Tōzai Taikō, has won or placed in every other major tournament numerous times. Last year, however, he was knocked out in the third round. Things did not go better for him this year, either. He made it through his first round match with a great *men* strike scored early on against Noda Atsushi (28, Aichi). Uchimura is so well known for his *kote* strike that you sometimes forget just how good his *men* is. In his second-round match against Kitaura Yūsuke, a 28-year-old 5-dan debutant from Nagasaki, Uchimura wasted no time in unleashing a trademark *kote* to take the lead. However, less than a minute later, Kitaura evened the match with a straight-down-the-middle *men* strike which Uchimura looked unprepared for and unable to respond to. The match continued and then around the three-minute mark, Uchimura went for *kote* but in the process left his own open. Kitaura was quick to react and took *kote* to progress to the third-round in his first AJKC.

It will be interesting to see if Uchimura tries to qualify next year. He really has nothing left to prove and his resume would be the envy of anyone. One more AJKF title would send him into clear second place behind Miyazaki Masahiro with six championships, and ahead of Chiba Masashi and Nishikawa Kiyonori, who also have three each. Uchimura will be 36 by the time of next year's championships, which is getting up there. This year, out of the 64 competitors, only four were that age or over. However, Miyazaki did get his sixth and final title when he was 36 in 1999, and Nishikawa Kiyonori secured his third and final title at the age of 39 in 1994.

Kendoka from Tokyo are usually very successful in the AJKC—10 competitors have taken 16 titles between them. However, with the exception of Shōdai Masahirō, the remaining three kenshi—Uchimura, Gonpei, and Shimoji Hidetsuna—all fell in the second round. Osaka usually fares well, too, but surprisingly all three of their competitors fell in the first round. Two of them were making their debut (Masuda Ryō and Tsuji Hideyuki) and Hagihara Toshiya was in his second AJKC.

All eyes in the Budokan were on Takenouchi as he stepped onto the floor for his first round match against the aforementioned Tsuji from Osaka. He won that with a *kote* in *enchō* to set up a second-round match with Tokyo's Gonpei. In the first round, Gonpei was drawn against the joint-oldest competitor, 39-year-old debutant Sone Takehito from Aichi, whom he defeated with *men* in *enchō*.

Despite being almost twice his age, Gonpei matched Takenouchi for speed and agility. He had what looked like a good shout for *kote* just before the end of regulation time, but the match continued. Soon after *enchō* started, Gonpei pressured Takenouchi, who was forced to retreat, and as he did so, Gonpei went for *kote*. Again, it looked solid and struck Takenouchi before he could make his *hiki-men* strike, but it was the latter that was awarded *ippon* to set up a third-round encounter with Katsumi Yōsuke (29) from Kanagawa police.

Katsumi, like Takenouchi, was only in his second AJKC. Katsumi had defeated Hokkaido's Ushirogi Akihito (31, 5-dan) in the first round with a *men* and then faced Yoneya in the second. That match turned out to be a *kote* festival with Katsumi taking the first, then Yoneya equalising before the former decided the match with another *kote* in *enchō*.

When Takenouchi and Katsumi met in the third round, I think that most people would have expected Takenouchi to win. As the defending AJKC champion, Takenouchi was the bigger name and he had also finished runner-up in the recent WKC individual championships. However,

Katsumi is an experienced competitor and has two WKC team championship titles to Takenouchi's one, and has won the Police Team Championships and the University Student Team Championships—a title that Takenouchi has won twice. Being a policeman, Katsumi has also been performing at a higher level than Takenouchi for a number of years. He also represents Kanagawa, one of the traditionally stronger prefectures. They were teammates at the 16th WKC and so must have known each other's kendo well.

The first real chance came at about the 1m40s mark—a *kote* for Katsumi as he lured Takenouchi into making a strike. After about 3m15s, after again pressuring Takenouchi, Katsumi scored a *de-gote* as his opponent went for *men*. The match came to life after that *ippon*, and Takenouchi became more aggressive but could not capitalise. This was his last entry as a student, as he will graduate in March 2016. We had heard that the University of Tsukuba were going to pull out all the stops to keep him there as a coach, but speaking to one of his *senpai* recently, I was informed that he will be joining the Tokyo police force. Whichever direction Takenouchi decides to head, this will certainly not be his last AJKC.

So what about the other two students, Umegatani and Sanada? Sanada beat 22-year-old Takeda Sōta, a policeman from Hyogo and his *senpai* from Kanoya. In the second round, Sanada faced R6-dan Sasagawa Hiroyuki (Saga) and lost in *enchō* to a *men* strike. Umegatani, on the other hand, fared much better.

In his debut AJKC, Umegatani made it all the way to the semi-final. On his way to meeting the eventual champion in the final four, he beat 6-dan Yamamoto Shōhei (Kyoto), 4-dan Satō Hirotaka (Chiba), 5-dan Osonoi Yūki (Ibaraki), and 5-dan Takami Masaru (Kanagawa)—all

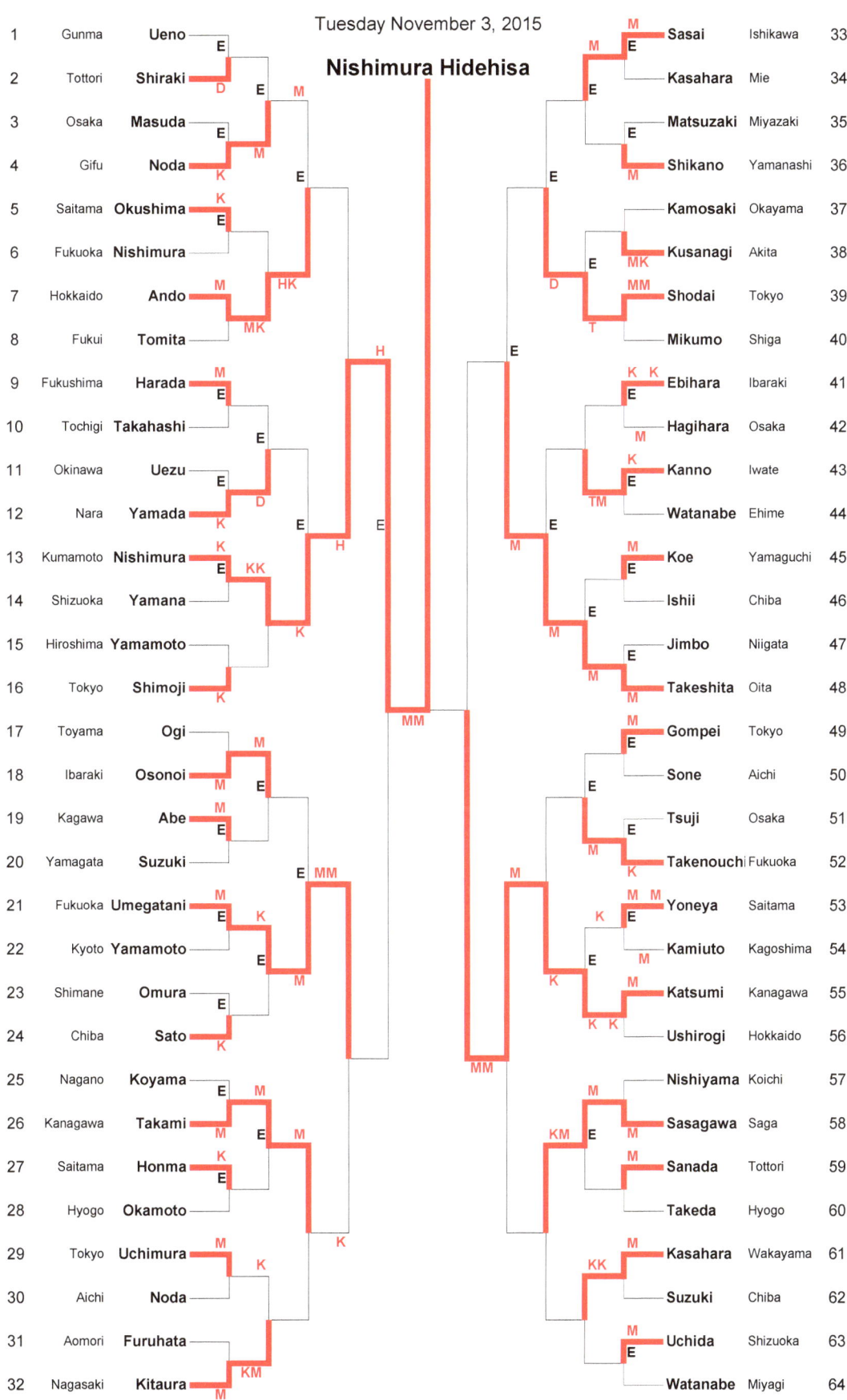

of them policemen with impressive competition records. (Interestingly, all of these competitors, like Umegatani, were making their debut.) Not at all bad for a 20-year-old, 3-dan student!

The pick of Umegatani's matches was the quarter-final against Takami. Umegatani conceded a *kote* after neat work by Takami, who enticed him into striking *kote*. Umegatani's strike lacked conviction and he did not close the *maai* enough. Takami then pounced to score a *kote ippon* after about 1m20s.

Matches at this stage of the AJKC are 10 minutes, so Takami could not see the duration out. Takami was attacking, seeking the *ippon* he needed to finish the match, and Umegatani to level it. As they were separating from *tsubazeriai*, Umegatani seized the opportunity and struck Takami's *shinai* at the *tsubamoto* with his *kensen*, knocking it down and scoring a *men ippon*. A short while later, Umegatani moved forward, quickly moving his *shinai* in a circular motion around his opponent's as he went. Takami was bamboozled and was forced back. As Takami stopped retreating and moved forward to strike *kote*, Umegatani launched a *men* strike that slow motion replays show did not made clean contact with the *men-buton*. Nevertheless, that finished the match and sent him into the semi-final for a showdown with Nishimura Hidehisa (Kumamoto). Incidentally, that was the only *ippon* that Umegatani conceded, and the only one of his matches that did not go into *enchō*.

During the AJKC, Kendo World commentator K8-dan Shigematsu Kimiaki-sensei mentioned on how this year's championships had a "fresh" feeling. Indeed, 29 of the 64 competitors were in their first AJKC, up on four from the previous year.

In the first quarter-final between Andō and Nishimura, the latter won through *hansoku-gachi* as he twice hooked his opponent's *shinai* from *ura* and knocked it to the ground. In quarter-final two Umegatani was victorious. In the third quarter-final, WKC team member Shōdai Masahiro (Tokyo), was defeated by Takeshita Yōhei (Oita). In the final quarter-final match Katsumi defeated Sasagawa Teppei (Saga) with a *men* strike.

In the first of the semi-finals, Nishimura faced Umegatani. This was Nishimura's second AJKC and he made it to this stage last year, too, but was ultimately defeated by Kunitomo. There was a lot of time spent in *tsubazeriai*. So much so, that the *shinpan* awarded both competitors a *hansoku*. This meant that Umegatani would have to be careful, as Nishimura won the quarter-final by twice

Final

making Andō drop his *shinai*. In the same manner, Nishimura was trying to hook his *shinai* around Umegatani's, but to no avail. *Enchō*. Nishimura made a great attempt at *kote*, but Umegatani countered with a *hiki-men*. Neither was given, but Nishimura careered into Umegatani to knock him out of the *shiai-jō*. Umegatani was consequently given a second *hansoku* giving Nishimura a *hansoku-gachi* for the second straight time.

The second semi-final was decided by two *ippon*—both *men* strikes from Katsumi. For the first *ippon*, Takeshita was pressing down on Katsumi's *shinai*. As he released and lowered his *shinai*, Katsumi changed from *omote* to *ura* to get his *shinai* around Takeshita's, which looked like it was heading for *kote*, and struck *men*. Soon after, in much the same way, Takeshita dropped his *kensen* and attempted *kote*, but Katsumi was quicker and struck *men* to book a place in the final.

The final was contested between Nishimura Hidehisa and Katsumi Yōsuke, who were both making only their second appearance in the AJKC. They probably knew each other's kendo well, as they were teammates at the WKC earlier in the year. Nishimura finished third in the WKC individual competition. Both competitors in this final were slightly more experienced than in the previous AJKC final. Having won both his quarter-final and semi-final matches by *hansoku-gachi*, Nishimura needed to put in a more convincing performance. He did not disappoint. About four minutes in, as

Katsumi was pushing down on his *shinai* from *omote*, Nishimura quickly dropped his *kensen*, changed to *ura* and struck *men*. Katsumi conceded a palpable point. Straight after the restart, Nishimura took a small step to the left to change to *ura*, moved his left foot forward and then kept on going and struck a *men* to finish the match in awesome style and become the 63rd All Japan Kendo Champion at 26 years of age.

Continuing from last year, it seems that the AJKC is getting younger, and that the guard is still changing. The future of the AJKC is certainly looking young and bright at the moment. It will be a brave person who tries to predict the results of the Japanese national championships next year…

The 63rd All Japan Kendo Championships in Numbers

By Yulin Zhuang

Kendo is a game of skill and difficult to quantify, but there is still value in looking at the numbers.

Time: There were a number of very long matches in the 63rd AJKC, with one bout lasting over 25 minutes. (See Fig. 1 and Fig. 2) Most matches took more than the regulation time to conclude, with only 17.5% of matches finishing in under five minutes. (See Fig. 3) Time was the deciding factor in more than 76% of the matches (See Fig. 4), which leads me to wonder how different the results might be if matches lasted for longer. By comparison, Olympic fencing matches are nine minutes long, with three one minute breaks.

Rank: So who survived until the later rounds? 5-dan is the most common *dan* grade, accounting for almost half of the participants, and three of the four semi-finalists. However, possessing a higher rank is no predictor of success, as none of the 6-dan or 7-dan kenshi made it past the quarter-finals. One precocious 3-dan, Umegatani Kakeru, made it all the way to the semi-final. (See Fig. 5)

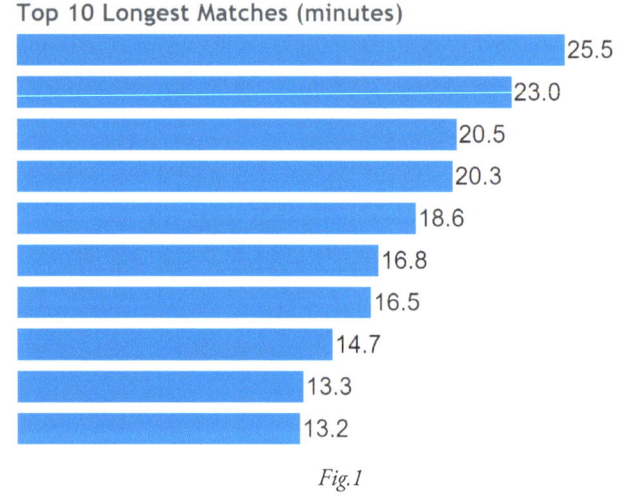

Fig.1

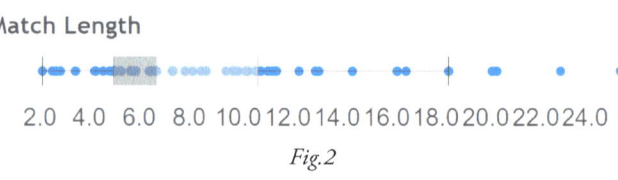

Fig.2

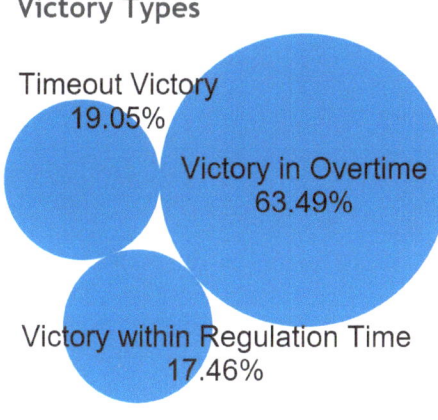

Fig.3

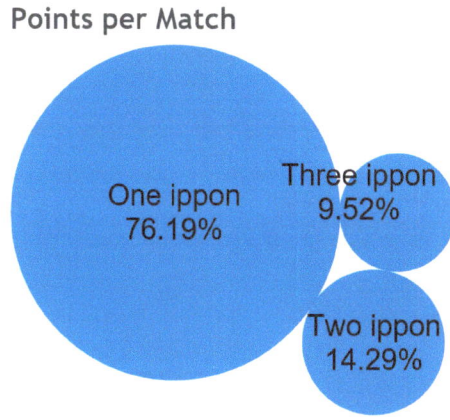

Fig.4

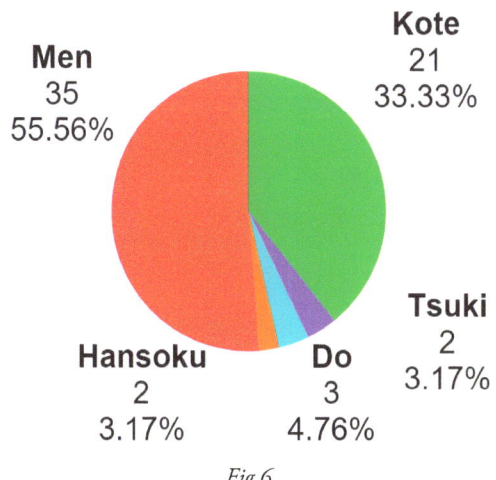

Fig.6

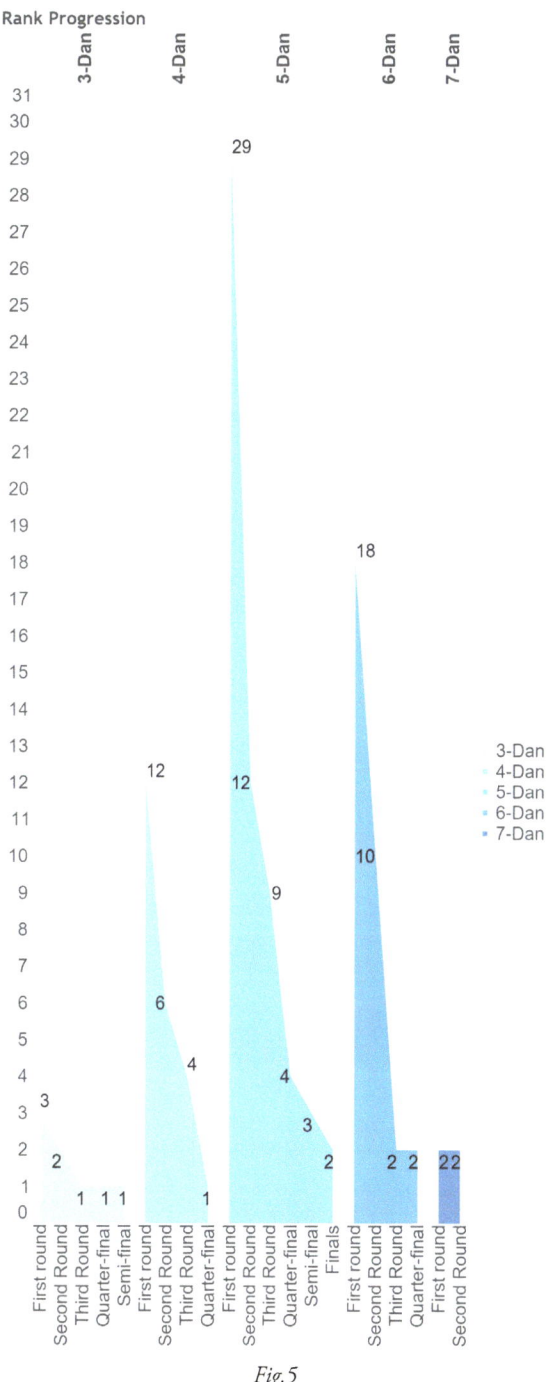

Fig.5

Points scored in the AJKC

It should be no surprise that *men* and *kote* were the most common *ippon* scored. Fig. 6 shows the total percentage of different *ippon* scored, but Fig. 7 shows the type, order, total points, and percentage of scored points across rounds. The size of each colour shows the total number of points of that type. Although the sample size is small, we see that *dō* and *tsuki* were never scored as the second or third point in a match, nor

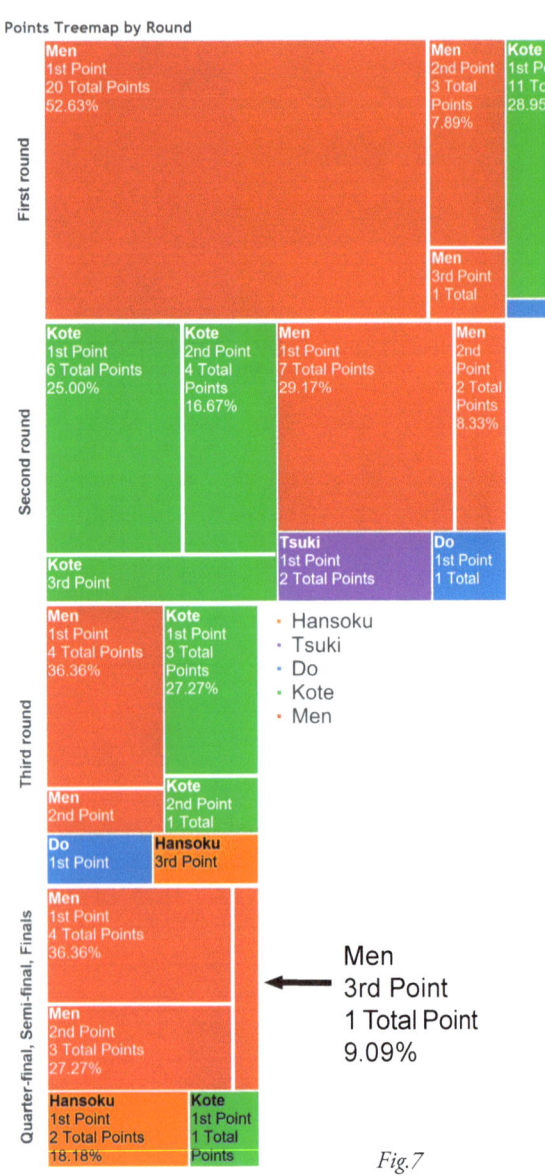

Fig.7

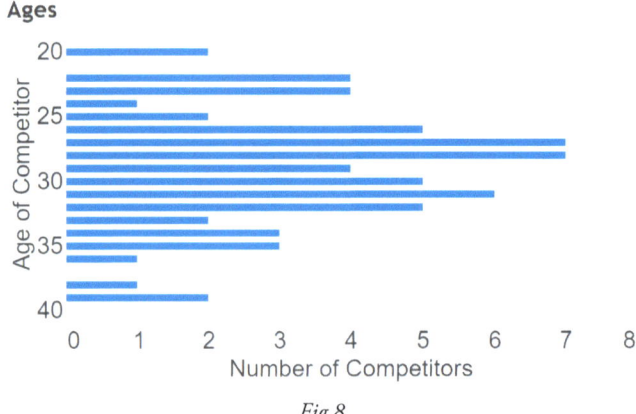

Fig.8

did we see any past the quarter-finals. This is possible evidence indicating a change in strategy towards more conservative strikes in the latter rounds, or that taking risks and attempting *dō* and *tsuki* strikes does not help you to progress to the later stages.

Age and Kendo

The median age of a participant in this year's AJKC was 28.5 years old. For comparison, the average age of Olympic athletes in 2012 was 26. The oldest competitor was Sone Takehito (39) and the youngest were Sanada Hiroyuki and Umegatani Kakeru, both just 20 years old. (See Fig. 8)

Profession and Kendo

So what do AJKC competitors do in real life? Well, the vast majority are policemen. Almost three quarters of the competitors—47 out of 64—are police officers. A further three are prison officers. Seven are teachers, and three are students. A mere four (6.3%) are regular company workers. (See Fig. 9)

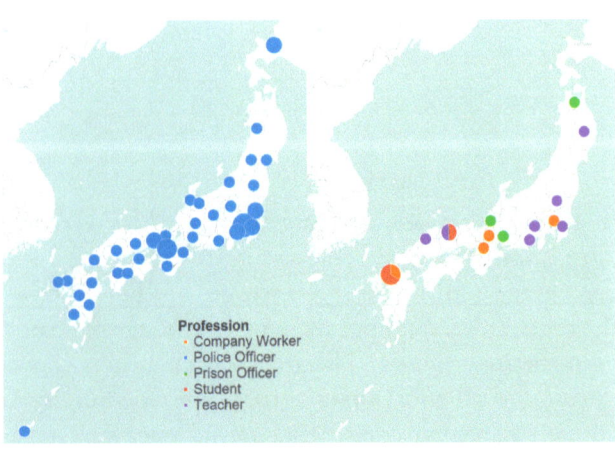

Fig.9

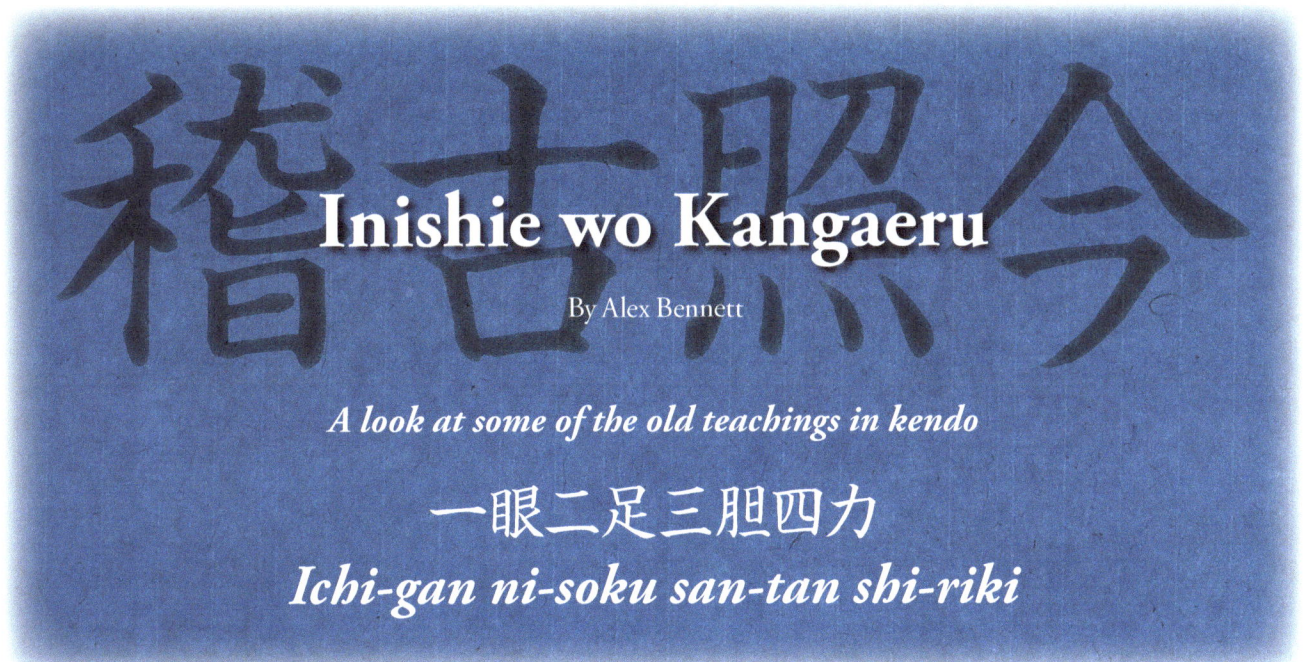

Inishie wo Kangaeru

By Alex Bennett

A look at some of the old teachings in kendo

一眼二足三胆四力
Ichi-gan ni-soku san-tan shi-riki

Ichi-gan

First, the eyes. What do you look at when facing off against an opponent? You look at their eyes, as they do yours. But more than that, you try to look through them, and sense what they are thinking. What is your opponent planning to do? What is his or her mental state? Scared? Confused? Confident? The eyes are used to observe the surface movements, and visualise what lies beyond. You observe their movement, and see their mind.

Ni-soku

Second, the legs. We're all told of the importance of footwork in kendo. We spend hours sliding across the floor with *okuri-ashi*, *suri-ashi*, *fumikomi-ashi*, and all the other *ashi*. People who strike with only their hands are corrected. Tall people are particularly prone to this because all they have to do is stick their arms out and the *shinai* hits the target, but the strike will lack the zing it needs to count. A strike made only with the hands will be discounted as being devoid of *ki-ken-tai-itchi*, the unison of spirit, sword and body. When watching others train, we are advised to look at the footwork of the strongest person in the group. Footwork is the foundation for any *waza*, and good footwork trumps all else.

San-tan

Third, guts. Some say that "kendo is beer", but that's a different kind of gut. There is the teaching of the "four sicknesses" or *shikai*: astonishment, fear, doubt, and hesitation. These are the debilitating mental conditions when faced with an opponent intent on hitting you. Having "*tan*" is to have the pluck, the courage, the guts to overcome these mental weaknesses and purge them from your heart, leaving a strong mind that remains unperturbed in the face of adversity.

Shi-riki

Fourth, strength. It is easy to mistake this as simply meaning physical power, but in fact it implies techniques (*waza*) and the strength to execute them. An old teaching suggests that *waza* are the flowers of the heart. It is also taught that *waza* are employed to correct the heart. Both are referring to the process of tempering the body to cultivate the mind. Techniques are the vehicle for this purpose, but without the first three elements, the techniques will never work.

In conclusion, this phrase outlines the four crucial components of a kendo *waza* in their order of importance: eyes, footwork, guts, and then technique. You face your opponent and observe their surface actions and their mind that dictates their movements, then launch your body in feet first with conviction and confidence to unleash a palpable blow. This is the correct process for striking in kendo.

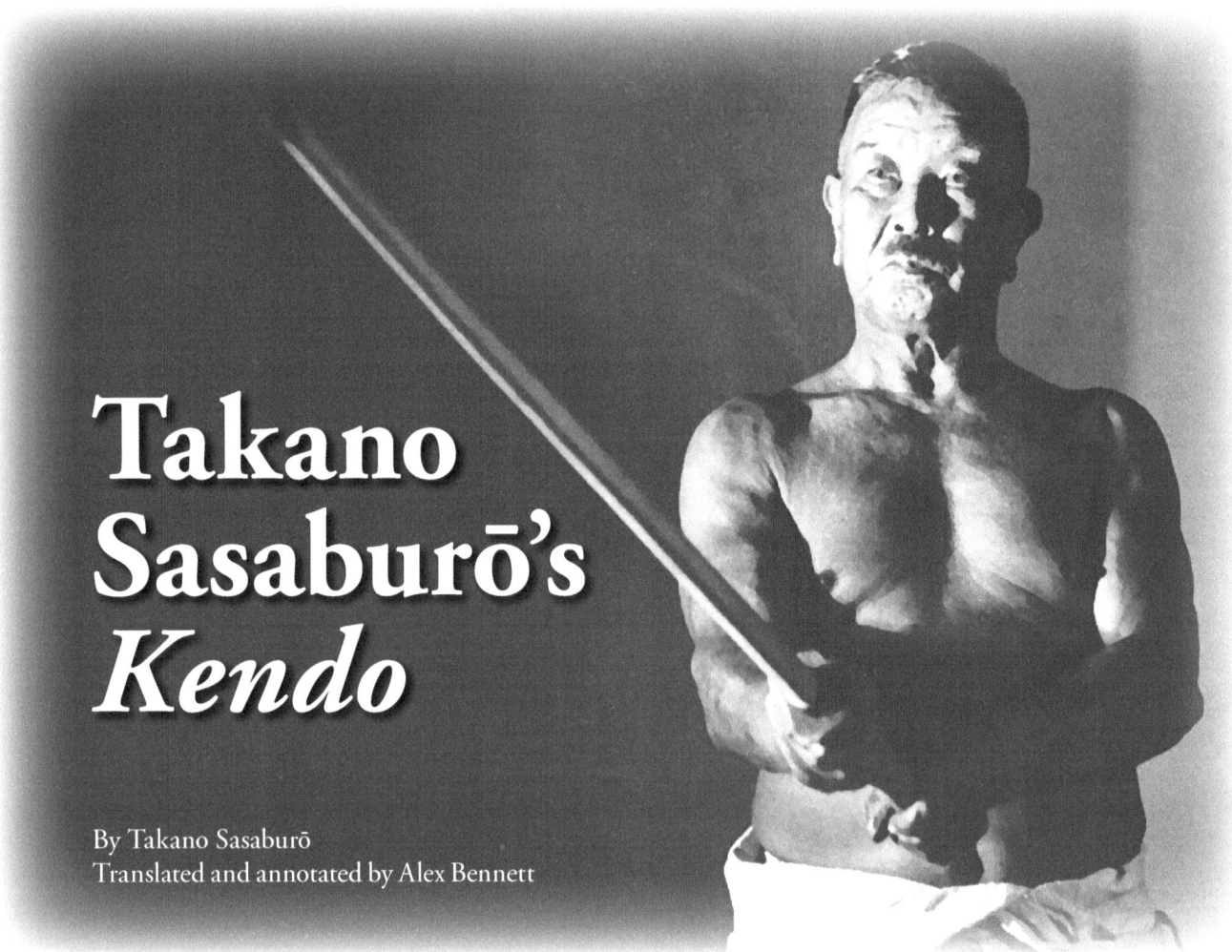

Takano Sasaburō's *Kendo*

By Takano Sasaburō
Translated and annotated by Alex Bennett

Takano Sasaburō (1862–1950) is considered one of the most influential pioneers of modern kendo. Commencing with his study of Nakanishi-ha Ittō-ryū *kenjutsu* at the age of 3, his remarkable skill in swordsmanship soon became apparent. He earned the nickname "little Tengu of Chichibu" after the mythical goblin-like creatures that excelled in martial arts. There were few who could match his talents, and he consistently defeated boys much older than himself. In 1879, he was pitted against well-known *kenjutsu* instructor Okada Sadagorō (1849–1895) at a local tournament. Takano assumed the rather unorthodox pose of one-handed *jōdan*. Okada took offence at his arrogance and proceeded to thrust mercilessly at his throat, handing Takano a painful defeat.

Ego and body battered and bruised, Takano decided to make his way to Tokyo to improve his skills and avenge his loss. By chance, Takano's grandfather had studied swordsmanship together with Yamaoka Tesshū's mentor, Asari Yoshiaki. With this connection, and an introduction from Shibata Emori, Sasaburō entered Tesshū's Shunpūkan dojo for a few months of gut-wrenchingly nasty training. Ready to take on his nemesis again, he requested a rematch, but was politely turned down by Okada.

Impressed by his single-minded resolve, Yamaoka Tesshū recommended him for an instructional position at the Keishichō (police) from 1886. In 1890, he established his own dojo, the Meishinkan. He was hired by Kanō Jigorō (founder of judo) to teach kendo at the Tokyo Higher Normal School (University of Tsukuba) from 1908, and simultaneously held numerous instruction positions at other universities including Waseda University, where Sasamori Junzō was one of his students. He was instrumental in developing the *dan* grading system for kendo, and was also a key member in the committee that created the Nihon Kendo Kata in 1912. His 1915 book simply titled *Kendō* was a *tour de force* in the creation of a uniform style for modern kendo, and is still thought of as a classic book by kendoka today. In this series of articles, I will translate Takano's book, and annotate the text to contextualise its ground-breaking content.

Chapter 1: The Objective of Kendo

Section 1—Kendo's Value

Kendo arose as a way for warriors to perfect their combat skills with the sword. The original objective was to develop technical ability and physical strength, and discipline the mind to attain victory in battle. Extending over seven centuries from the Genpei era[1] through to the end of the Tokugawa period (1603–1868), the mantle of power in Japan was controlled by the shogun, regents, and the various daimyo lords throughout the country. They were able to do this because of their ability to use arms.

As professional men-at-arms, the politically dominant samurai class dedicated considerable time and effort in honing their martial prowess. Swordsmanship was considered to be a crucial skill for warriors of all ranks. It was necessary on the battlefield, and was also indispensable for self-defence in the course of daily life. Of all the weapons, the sword was among the most important, and the quest to master its art led to a realm of technical exquisiteness. The practice of swordsmanship incorporated ceremonial protocols and various customs that continually evolved over many centuries. Swordsmanship was important not only for practical purposes, but also for developing the mental fortitude needed to prevail in combat. By virtue of this, swordsmanship was also recognised as an excellent vehicle in the quest for self-perfection.

Japanese society underwent radical changes after the Meiji Restoration (1868). Warrior society was dismantled from the shogun down, and all four of the traditional classes (warriors, farmers, artisans, merchants) were afforded the same rights as citizens of Japan. Following the reconstruction of Japan's military system, traditional martial arts as a pursuit for self-cultivation fell by the wayside. What was once an important duty for samurai—training morning and night in horsemanship (*bajutsu*), archery (*kyūjutsu*), spearmanship (*sōjutsu*), and so on—became little more than a divertissement barely kept alive by a few diehards. From around the beginning of the Meiji period (1868–1912) enthusiasm for the martial arts went into decline.

Kendo was then linked with Western-styled military swordsmanship (*guntō-jutsu*) and bayonet practice (*jūkenjutsu*). Although its practical value was acknowledged, traditional swordsmanship it was not considered as useful or relevant as it was in the feudal era. Some people saw kendo as a military exercise with some benefits in terms of health, whereas others ridiculed it as being little more than an outdated relic from a past era. This was a terrible underestimation of kendo's worth. To reiterate, through centuries of rigorous training and refinement by countless skilled swordsmen, kendo transformed into a means for developing body and mind, and proved to be an excellent path for personal cultivation among samurai. "Personal development" in this sense was not restricted to preparing for war. It encompassed nurturing the essence of the Japanese people (*Yamato damashii*), which for centuries has been replete with the martial spirit. This martial spirit is known as "bushido", and can be cultivated through the study of kendo. This in turn encourages patriotism and loyalty, builds the stamina necessary to engage in all manner of productive activities, and conveys the ideal temperament for Japanese citizens.

This is why kendo occupies a special place in Japan compared to other popular sports and paths. I believe that the value of kendo now lies in the ongoing advancement of Japan and its people. The immense relevance of kendo can hardly be expressed in a few words, but in a nutshell its meaning can be summarised in the phrase "*shinshin-tanren*"; to "anneal the body and mind".

Section 2—Kendo and Annealing the Body and Mind

Many have espoused the virtues of kendo for strengthening body and mind, but few have stopped to judiciously analyse exactly how and why. Non-practitioners typically disregard the enthusiastic ramblings of kendo aficionados. Notwithstanding, the holistic benefits of kendo are crucial to its social significance, and warrant careful consideration.

The purpose of games and physical exercise is to facilitate physical growth, improve organ function and overall well-being, and build athletic dexterity and coordination. In the case of callisthenics, each one of the drills has been rationally conceived, and is undoubtedly of benefit if done properly.

Primary school pupils undergo a suitable regime of physical exercise and learn various games. When they leave the school gates, however, everything changes. The child might not be keen to take up an extracurricular activity. Even if a sport is of interest, the environment for meaningful participation may be lacking, meaning that

---
[1] Twelfth century.

Takano Sasaburō instructing students at the Tokyo Higher Normal School.

the expected results are rarely achieved.

With kendo, anyone can join in and give it their all regardless of age, financial means, cold or hot weather, or whether it is day or night. Kendo gets the blood circulating, improves digestion, stimulates the organs, and cultivates coordination and stamina. Surviving the cold of winter or the heat of summer, overcoming the discomfort and fatigue of harsh training, enduring the unendurable and cultivating lionhearted grit is all part of kendo training. There is nothing that can match kendo in terms of forging strength in body and heart. Furthermore, kendo is not a temporary form of exercise. It is a perpetual path with the dual purpose of galvanising the body and polishing the mind. The more one does kendo, the more interesting it becomes, and it can be pursued throughout one's lifetime.

Posture is central in kendo. One of the rewards of doing kendo is that it rectifies posture thereby facilitating a robust constitution, dexterity, and ample staying power. This in turn has clear benefits both directly and indirectly for the soul. In addition, the underpinning spirit of bushido and the rigorous training that epitomises kendo aids in nurturing the virtues of vivaciousness, fortitude, perseverance, endurance, diligence, and good temperament. The practitioner also learns to behave courteously, and to act appropriately in front of one's mentors and peers.

Kendo aids in fostering a wide range of sensibilities. One must be flexible enough to adopt to an endless series of changes when competing. Staying within the rules, the kendo competitor carefully observes the physical and mental state of the opponent in search of a weakness, or indeed to induce one. The encounter is not unfair or cowardly in the slightest. In fact, just behaviour is emphasised in bouts, and the practitioner learns an acute sense of right and wrong. Kendo also stimulates confidence, and the practitioner becomes magnanimous and tolerant of others. This explanation is not fanciful; these virtues and more are fostered over many years of training. The benefits I list here are merely the most obvious ones.

Many sports and games popular in Japan focus on enjoyment or physical benefits, but few can claim to be useful in shaping a strong mind. In terms of moral development, theoretical concepts are hardly satisfactory; only actual participation can bring tangible results. To this end, the intrinsic value of kendo is in that is not just taught or learned for a limited time—it is a continual process of study that never ends.

For the sake of expedience, I will outline the physical and mental aspects of training separately. It goes without saying that these two elements go hand-in-hand, and are not unconnected. A vivacious spirit burgeons through correcting posture and honing motor skills while abiding by the protocols of etiquette. Furthermore, promotion of good manners and a vivacious spirit in turn serves to promote correct posture and deftness movement. It is impossible to rectify posture if one cares not about etiquette and propriety. One's movement will become lethargic, and one's mind will be dull. Strength of body augments discipline, endurance, diligence, and strong character; and conversely, is maintained through discipline and endurance. In this way, standing heedfully with sword in hand, the practitioner is able to keenly sense subtle changes in the opponent's eyes, posture, arms, and sword tip. This facilitates the ability to react instantaneously and appropriately with nimbleness and resolve. The sequence of engagement in kendo is a model for implementing one's intentions, and provides a model for the fundaments of action in daily life.

Sincerity is essential when dealing with various worldly matters. Nothing needs to be feared in the world if one is sincere. Kendo revolves around this premise, and is requisite for fostering an immovable spirit and technical ability. Apart from the visible aspects of kendo such as the techniques, the invisible aspect of mental application is crucial. In the days of yore, famous swordsmen successfully accessed the secrets of swordsmanship through the teachings of Zen Buddhism. Entering the highest realm in swordsmanship and Zen are essentially the same. Without an enlightened mind, one will never fully understand the mysteries of kendo. This is the mind that is unsullied, serene, and selfless, and which does not distinguish

Dai-Nippon Butokukai Teikoku Kendo Kata committee members. Front row from the left - Tsuji Shinpei, Negishi Shingorō. Back row from right - Monna Tadashi, Naitō Takaharu, Takano Sasaburō.

between life and death. It is unfettered and able to cope with any change. It is the mind that can defeat one or one-hundred enemies without faltering.

Most pursuits referred to as "ways" seek the same enlightened state. Among them, kendo shines as one of pure magnificence. Still, entry into the supreme realm cannot be achieved without years of discipline. It can never be reached in a day or a night. One will reap six months' worth of benefits from six months of training; one year's worth of benefits from one year of training. Results will come if one is relentless; and the more one puts into it, the more one gets out of it. In other words, the focus of kendo is not simply to **acquire** techniques to win contests; it is to forge the body and mind *through* the acquisition of techniques. This point must not be forgotten.

Section 3—Bushido and Kendo

Kendo is a superb invention of Japan, and is inextricably linked to the Yamato spirit, or bushido—the soul of the Japanese people. All of the powerful countries of the world advanced through the strength of arms. No country, however, has managed to successfully maintain a constantly high calibre in its martial affairs and expand its interests while repelling the threat of foreign incursion to the extent that Japan has. One only has to look at the history of Japan over the last 2,500 years, from the time when Emperor Kanmu (737–806) unified the country until our great victory in the Russo-Japanese War (1905). This is testament to the loyalty, patriotism, and military prowess that symbolises our country. As the spiritual foundation of the Japanese, bushido is surely one of our greatest assets.

Takano Sasaburō (left) demonstrating kata with Nakayama Hakudō.

Bushido has been a part of the Japanese psyche since ancient times. A valorous and virile spirit, reverence for the imperial family, and veneration of our ancestors always characterised the Japanese people. This trait became more pronounced near the end of the Fujiwara hegemony during the Heian period (794–1185), after which warriors rose to prominence with the gradual decline of central authority. In the various regions throughout Japan, warrior chieftains held absolute power over their vassals, who in turn devoted themselves to a relationship of fealty—considered to be the finest virtue of a warrior.

The warrior epoch was turbulent and unpredictable. The spoils of war went to those with military strength, and those without were vanquished. The only way a vassal could demonstrate his sense of loyalty was through valour in the throes of battle. To this end, warriors fought bravely with little regard for their own safety, and dying in front of the master's horse was lauded as the highest form of honour. It was because of such uncertainty that the ideal of loyalty and an indomitable martial spirit became the cornerstone of morality in the way of the warrior. This is bushido.

The only way to embody bushido was through learning and perfecting the military arts of mounted archery, sword, and the pike. Bushido and *bujutsu* represent both sides of a coin, and one cannot go without the other. *Bujutsu* received its spirit and ideals from bushido, and evolved into a canon with refined protocols and form. As an ideal, bushido was able to thrive though arduous training in the martial arts.

The warrior mastered several military arts including the bow, horse, sword and pike. Each was a cog in the bushido tradition, but kendo must surely be viewed as the representative art of the samurai. The Japanese have revered swords since ancient times. A sword is included in the three items of the imperial regalia, and all warrior houses from the shogun down to the rank-and-file treasured swords as family heirlooms. It stands to reason that swordsmanship was widespread given that the sword was afforded so much respect. Kendo was not only studied by members of the warrior caste, but was also popular among commoners, and the clash of *shinai* could be heard throughout the land. Its popularity has continued through to the present day.

Bushido and kendo evolved together in special social circumstances, but the spiritual underpinning has long been a part of the Japanese mentality. Kendo is something that must never be lost in the constant changes in society and its systems. The spirit of bushido became more defined with improved education during the Tokugawa period. The fundaments of bushido are demonstrated in loyalty, valour, fidelity to one's principles, a sense of shame, politeness, honour and character, valuing one's name, and benevolence. These characteristics constitute the morality of Japan's polity and people.

True to these ideals, the Japanese people continue to progress as a nation, and will grow further in the modern world under the guiding light of bushido. There is nothing that can surpass the spirit of bushido. The Japanese work day and night, and esteem the "Imperial Rescript on Education"[2] and the "Imperial Rescript to Soldiers and Sailors"[3] promulgated by His Royal Highness Emperor Meiji. As long as bushido is embraced, Japan's national prestige will grow evermore. There is more than one way to impart the teachings of bushido, but from an historical perspective, the solemn and rigorous practice of kendo is

---

2　The "Imperial Rescript on Education was signed by Emperor Meiji on October 30, 1890. It stipulated official policy on the guiding principles of education. All students were expected to memorise the text as their duty as a Japanese citizen and loyal subject of the emperor. These passages may seem to exceedingly nationalistic, but the period in which the book was written should be remembered. One of the Takano's goals, apart from explaining the mechanics of kendo in the later chapters, was to set the tone for why (Japanese) people should study it. Such rhetoric was common in the early 1900s as Japan tried to establish itself on the international stage while moulding a modern national identity.

3　The "Imperial Rescript to Soldiers and Sailors" was the official ethical guideline implemented for Japan's modernised military, and was promulgated on January 4, 1882. It became the most important document in the development of the Imperial Japanese Army and Navy until the end of the Second World War, and all military personnel were required to memorise the content.

undoubtedly the finest.

When compared with the powerful nations of the world, there are many areas in which the Japanese seem to be retrograde. This is evident when we look at our history, but is nothing to be ashamed of. What is necessary now is to reset our focus on future development. If an individual is not endowed with natural talents and has not inherited financial means, all is not lost. With a resolute mind, strong body, and perseverance, success can be achieved in all walks of life even with only limited education and skills. Even as the gap separating Japan from the other great nations of the world closes, it behoves each citizen to continue striving to cultivate a determined mind, physical robustness, and to keep working hard to excel on all fronts. As I have already stated, kendo is undeniably one of the best methods to anneal the mind and body for such ends.

Section 4—The Practical Benefits of Kendo

Teachers, practitioners, and supporters of kendo tout its physical, mental and moral merits, but few reference its practical attributes. The techniques of kendo should not be overlooked. With advances in technology, the principle weapon in the armed forces, especially infantry, is the gun. Most confrontations involve fighting with guns, but the experience of the Russo-Japanese War showed that cold steel was in fact a decisive factor in battle. In this sense, strength of mind and body, and technical adeptness fostered through kendo training can be directly applied to military swordsmanship (*guntōjutsu*) and bayonet training (*jūkenjutsu*). With the present-day climate in which "each citizen has an obligation to fight for the country", the practical applicability of kendo is particularly pertinent, especially in a system that relies on reservists.

Notwithstanding, there is an influential line of thought that asks, "Even if one learns kendo, gets conscripted and drafted into the army, NCOs and below only have bayonets at the front. So, what is the point of learning kendo?" In response to such naysayers, General Nogi Maresuke (1814–1912) once said:

> It is not the case at all [that kendo training is superfluous]. Men who have studied kendo are rich in pluck and drive, and excel in bayonet training, as all will attest to. That is not all. They have confidence, and can see the right timing to exploit an enemy's weakness. There are many benefits to be had. During the war with Russia, it was clear that those who had studied *gekken* and *jūjutsu* were superior in terms of mettle and motivation compared to those who had not. They fought well in combat, and in addition to inspiring others, they performed in exemplary fashion when called upon to act independently in such duties as reconnaissance. (General Nogi's "*Bushidō mondō*")

If it is just a matter of practicality, then some may argue that it would be better to do *jūkenjutsu* rather than kendo. This argument does have merit. It would be acceptable to choose *jūkenjutsu* if it had the same advantages in forging physical and mental dexterity as kendo, but it does not measure up at all in this regard. The main reasons are as follows:

- The replica wooden rifle (*mokujū*) is heavy, and requires brute strength to wield it, quickly causing fatigue.
- The technical repertoire is limited and comparatively one-dimensional, meaning that it is not conducive to a full body workout. For these two reasons, the activity is not suitable for younger boys.
- As the techniques are simple, it is not useful for cultivating delicate movement and the subtle mental insights that come with it.
- Thus, *jūkenjutsu* lacks the interest that kendo holds.

There are many more reasons that could be iterated, but I will refrain from doing so here. When one tries to apply the mind and techniques learned in *jūkenjutsu* to kendo, the level is extremely low; whereas, if one transfers the lessons learned in kendo to *jūkenjutsu*, clearly the rewards are immense.

"Chikushōshin wo sare"
(Purge oneself of the animal mind.)

Harigaya Sekiun (1593–1662), founder of the Mujūshinken-ryū (Sekiun-ryū). His teaching of "*ainuke*" (mutual passing) is famous.

"Many martial arts draw on the powers of animals—the fury of a lion, nimbleness of a butterfly, agility of a monkey… The characteristics of Harigaya Sekiun's teachings were to completely forget about winning or losing the contest, and just seek a higher plain in one's natural state, not emulating animals. Seek the aiuchi (mutual strike)."

The 1620s–40s were a golden era for swordsmanship. There are many famous swordsmen from this period, and one man in particular stands out as a truly bizarre, but brilliant specimen—Harigaya Sekiun, born in a village in Kōzuke Harigaya. The enlightened state that he attained was premised on the idea of becoming oblivious to the outcome of the encounter. There is nothing particularly unique about this idea, but Sekiun took it to another level. He advocated the ideal of going for a draw through *aiuchi* (simultaneous strike)!

Of course, it goes without saying that swordsmen studied their craft to master techniques to kill without getting killed in the process. In this sense, the notion that a mutual strike is the objective is strange to say the least. An old poem advises, "Sacrificing the self (*sutemi*) brings the best chance for success." But, this is simply the mindset for winning, and is very different to what Sekiun was championing. His ideal was not a 'mindset'; it was an imperative that would result in certain death. How does one reconcile this blatantly self-destructive attitude? One would think his school would have been remarkably short-lived!

"There are three occasions where the warrior draws his sword: in battle, at the behest of one's lord, or in a sudden outbreak of violence. And in all cases, it is not shameful

SWORDS OF WISDOM

By
ALEX BENNETT
Based on the book
"KENSHI NO MEIGON" (1998)
by the late Tobe Shinjūrō
Used with author's permission.

whatsoever if the end result is a mutual slaying." A mutual, simultaneous strike might seem like a simple matter of two people attacking at the same time. According to Sekiun, it required becoming one with the opponent, and an acceptance that life and death are the same. To access such a high plain of enlightened indifference is not simple by any stretch of the imagination. If one can achieve this, Sekiun advised, one can become a master worthy of "*ainuke*"—not "mutual striking" but "mutual passing".

Ainuke is indeed a paradoxical term. Sekiun was apparently illiterate, and must have come up with the idea through experience and some kind of intense, combat induced epiphany. It was undoubtedly a play on the word *aiuchi* (mutual strike) but the philosophy is far more profound. "In other schools, swordsmanship can be summed up in three categories: beat the weak, lose to the strong, or men of equal skill settlingwith a simultaneous strike. In my school, when two enlightened swordsmen face off, knowing that they can't win the confrontation, it ends in a draw. This is '*ainuke*'. My school is created on sagacious principles. There is only one sage in each era, so if two should meet by chance, then *ainuke* is the inevitable conclusion." Make sense?

Sekiun's teacher was Ogasawara Nagaharu. Nagaharu learned the art of the sword under Okudaira Kyūgasai, a top student of the legendary Kamiizumi Ise-no-Kami of the Shinkage-ryū. Nagaharu also ranked highly on the 'weird scale', and headed over to China to gain some respite from the incessant war in Japan. While there, he met a martial artist of high pedigree who taught him the art of the glaive. Nagaharu taught his Chinese friend Japanese swordsmanship in return. When he returned to Japan, he had a new secret martial art to show off to his cronies. Nobody knows what the technique he called "*hassun no enkin*" was. It may have been a weapon rather than a technique. Anybody who has seen a demonstration of Chinese martial arts will know how dynamic, even acrobatic, they are. Nagaharu's new style was a sight to behold with its ostentatious leaps and turns. He soon made a name for himself, and apparently amassed a following of 3,000 students. Among them was Sekiun, but he too stood out with his eccentricity. Nagaharu certainly had the skill and won 52 duels.

Still, Sekiun had his doubts about standard interpretations of swordsmanship, especially after commencing with the study of Zen under Kohaku Oshō at the Ryōkōji Temple. This experience altered his perception of the martial arts and life. He started to think that the swordsmanship he had studied hitherto under such reputable masters was in fact fraudulent. Jumping, blocking, and spinning out of danger seemed to be totally missing the point. These were the movements of beasts! "Be natural and purge yourself of the animal mind." This is what Sekiun discovered. In other words, *ainuke* is only attainable when one leaves animal impersonations behind—that is, not incorporating the instinctual behavior of beasts for the sake of survival.

This, Sekiun realised, was the supreme level of swordsmanship, and the highest level of humanity. Go straight in for the kill, he beseeched, without avoiding the oncoming enemy strike. If it results in *aiuchi*, then so be it. Both dead. If one survives long enough, a sage one will become; sensing this, people will avoid confrontation. If another sage happens along, both will know straight away that Mutually Assured Destruction is the only outcome, so they pass each other by. That is the meaning of *ainuke*.

KENDO FOR ADULTS

By Hatano Toshio (Courtesy of *Kendo Nihon*)
Translated by Alex Bennett

Hatano Toshio-sensei was born in January 1945 in Musashi Murayama, Tokyo. After graduating from Kokushikan High School and Nihon University, he became a salaryman for a few years before establishing the Nanbudō Kendōgu shop in 1971. He passed the 8-dan exam on his second attempt in 1994. He serves as an advisor for the West Tokyo Kendo Federation, and is Suruga University Kendo Club Shihan, Musashi Murayama City Kendo Federation president, and leader of the Kinryūkan Dojo.

Part 3: Kaeshi-dō for a Long Kendo Life

What is your take on "*seme*"? Many people seem to think that *seme* is simply "to go forth and strike", but this is not the case. *Seme* boils down to how much you can invoke a reaction in your opponent. If you have strong *seme*, your opponent will react all the more. Conversely, it means that your *seme* is weak if your opponent does not move when you apply pressure.

Distance is extremely important when pressurising your opponent. If you assail your opponent from a distance that is impossible to strike from, your opponent won't budge no matter how primed you are to attack. On the other hand, that doesn't mean that you should get in too close either, as you will leave yourself open by doing so. It is precisely because pressure is applied from the one-step one-strike interval (*issoku-ittō-no-maai*) that the opponent will try to negate the pressure by lifting their hands.

Why is *seme* even necessary? What should you be looking to do? Let me explain with the example of getting on a train and observing the person facing you. "How old is this person? Judging by his clothes, he is probably high up in his company. His shoes and belt look expensive. He's obviously a stickler for detail and quite fashion conscious…." This is the sort of information you can glean about a person if you look carefully, but it is not so easy to work out his personality. You can only really work this out by talking with him. The deeper the conversation, the more you learn about his character.

Kendo is exactly the same. You can understand a few things about your opponent through observation. For example, it is safe to assume that he or she is quite experienced if tidy in appearance. Nevertheless, you won't know straight away what kind of *waza* they use, or the style of kendo that they do. Furthermore, you won't know how they will react to your kendo, so unleashing a *waza* and just hoping for the best is not an option.

求めずに 剣道良くなる 道理なし
Motomezu ni Kendō yoku naru Dōri nashi
Without 'seeking' / Improvement in kendo / Is Unreasonable

To use baseball as an analogy, it's the same as a pitcher suddenly throwing an easy-to-slug pitch right up the middle; if the pitcher doesn't know what the batter is aiming for, nine times out of ten such a throw will be smashed into the stands by a pro. In the case of kendo, simply jumping in without knowing the style of kendo one's opponent does, or how they will react, will result in you being smashed into the stands. This is why *seme* is necessary. Your opponent may respond in a number of ways when you apply pressure: suppress from above, step back and keep their distance, stay put and endure… You must work out the appropriate *waza* to apply based on their reaction.

Successful *kaeshi-dō* depends on *shinai* trajectory

Seme is crucial, even for *go-no-sen* techniques—counter strikes—such as *kaeshi-dō*. *Go-no-sen* techniques are not about waiting for your opponent to strike and then reacting. Success comes from applying pressure (*seme*), forcing a move, and then counter striking. If you have strong *seme*, it becomes very uncomfortable for the opponent who then feels compelled to do something.

As one gets older, it becomes increasingly difficult to take on younger kenshi using off-the-line "*sen*" techniques because of the disparity in speed and agility. Even if you would have reached the target in your younger days, attempting *men* against a tall opponent may not be easy (or even possible) anymore. If you wish to enjoy kendo into your old age, you need to master techniques where your opponent is cajoled into making a move.

In this sense, *go-no-sen waza* become progressively important, but it is good to start learning them properly when you are young. One representative *go-no-sen* technique is *kaeshi-dō*. Children are often good at scoring *nuki-dō*, but looking at the All Japan Kendo Championships or the Hachidan Taikai, *nuki-dō* hardly features at all. Instead, *kaeshi-dō* techniques are more prominent. This is why I feel it is better to teach *kaeshi-dō* to children from the outset. I teach this technique to primary school pupils from ten years-of-age and up.

When I see skilled high school students battling it out at the Inter-High level, it seems apparent to me that most of them are unable to implement *kaeshi-dō* properly. They have probably only learned how to do *nuki-dō*, and nobody has bothered to teach them the subtleties of *kaeshi-dō*. This is clear after the strike as the *shinai* ends up in a very high position. The trajectory of the *shinai* when executing *kaeshi-dō* is high to low.

This is a common method for striking *kaeshi-dō* in high school level matches. The *shinai* is received above the head, the counterstrike cuts down, but the *shinai* is retuned to a high position once again at the end of the movement (see photos below). From the standpoint of *tōhō* (katana usage), finishing a *kaeshi-dō* technique this way would be impossible.

With *men-kaeshi-dō*, the *shinai* is received in a high position, so the ensuing strike to *dō* should travel a diagonal path from high to low, not the other way around. This suggests that the strike is being made with the side of the *shinai*, and the *hasuji* (angle of the blade) is incorrect. This happens because people practise *kaeshi-dō* the same as they do *nuki-dō*. Remember, the trajectory for *kaeshi-dō* is high→low. It is the opposite of *nuki-dō* (low→high).

An important point for successful kaeshi-dō is striking high to low.

This is the same striking motion from the front.

This is Orikasa-san's kaeshi-dō strike. The resulting dō strike is cramped and indecisive because of the position of his hands in the initial block.

I am the Shihan for Surugadai University Kendo Club. When I instruct the students there, I ask them to strike *kaeshi-dō* without telling them what they are doing wrong. They will not get it right no matter how many times they go through the exercise. They have no idea that they have been doing it wrong for so long. I then advise them that the way they are using the *shinai* runs counter to the principles of the sword, and that their technique for *kaeshi-dō* is fundamentally flawed. It doesn't take them long to fix the problem once they know the reasoning behind their mistake.

Another important factor in striking *kaeshi-dō* is the positioning of the hands when receiving the *men* strike, and *tenouchi*. My assistant for this section is Orikasa Tamaoki. He was not very good at *kaeshi-dō*, and the first problem was his hand positioning when receiving the *men*.

Hit the opponent's shinai sharply with arms extended in the centre as if to deflect it upward.

If your hands are pulled in as you block, the opponent will be too close, and it will be difficult to strike the correct section of the dō (left photo). Pushing your arms out gives you more elbowroom to strike accurately and effectively (right photo).

Hand positioning is crucial in striking *kaeshi-dō* successfully. Receiving the strike so close to the head means that the opponent is too close, and becomes even closer in the time is takes to bring the *shinai* down to strike *dō*. Instead of striking *migi-dō* (right side of the *dō*) the *shinai* will inevitably make contact with the stomach in the front. In this way, people have trouble with *kaeshi-dō* because their arm is bent when blocking, and the attacker ends up too close to strike properly.

When receiving the *men*, be sure to have your arms extended in front rather than pulled back. Don't think of it as "receiving"; rather, you are "hitting" their *shinai* as it comes in. This way, the opponent's *shinai* will be deflected up and knocked off the centreline. A rapid downward cutting motion is crucial after the *shinai* clash. This is facilitated by having your arms extended; the cut down will be all the more sharper by thrusting your arms out to receive the *men*.

The hips are turned slightly to the left when hitting the opponent's *shinai* up with the block. That way, the cut down to the right will be naturally stronger and more straightforward. This is precisely what is meant by "striking with your hips" (*koshi de utsu*). I often see others receiving the initial blow to *men* with their hips turned to the right. This means that their hips cannot be utilised properly in the strike. The strike will be completed with the hands only, and will be weak as a result.

To turn your hips in the strike requires proper use of the knees. If you have watched a baseball player at the plate, you will notice that his knees are slightly bent as he takes his batting stance. This is because it is impossible to turn your hips adequately when standing tall. With legs bent at the knees, the batter is able to generate an almighty swing and hit the ball with more vigour. To bend the knees when attempting *kaeshi-dō*, you must drop your centre of gravity the instant the *shinai* come into contact.

This can be achieved through widening your stance by moving the right foot forward. If you don't move your right foot as you receive the *men* strike, you will find it difficult to generate momentum in your midriff.

I point my toes slightly inward as I move my right foot out. Like baseball, you need a decent backswing to get power in the strike. By turning my toes inward, I feel that I am producing enough of a backswing to make the strike to *dō* powerful. Turning your hips is also important when striking *gyaku-dō*; the hips turn to the right when receiving the *men* strike, and then the *shinai* is brought down to strike *dō* as the hips are returned to the left. In both cases of left or right *dō* strikes, the *shinai* should be on a 45° angle when contact is made. This angle is crucial. When practising *kaeshi-dō*, just repeat the *kaeshi* portion over and over to start with if you have difficulty blocking and striking in one smooth motion.

Hatano-sensei scoring men-kaeshi-dō against his opponent at the 2011 Kyoto Taikai.

Turn the wrists and receive with the opposite *shinogi*

I notice that many people—8-dan sensei included—leave their *shinai* at the *dō* position and simply move to the right. If the *dō* strike is completed with the appropriate amount of power, the wrists should flick forward, and the *kensen* naturally continues through on a forward course. When I block *men* strikes, I practise turning my wrists as much as possible. The standard method for receiving a strike is with the palms of your hands directed toward the opponent. I go a step further than that and end up with the back of my hands facing the opponent. To strike

dō from this position means that you have to turn your wrists back effectively. This in turn results in more power being generated in the strike.

The way I practise the *kaeshi* movement is by twisting my wrists around even further to reveal the top of my hands to the opponent. Some criticise this movement because they see it as essentially blocking with the cutting edge of the blade. This is not the intention; I am attempting to receive the strike with the *shinogi* (blade side) on the opposite side of the *shinai*.

Finally, the most important thing to strike *kaeshi-dō* suc-

The standard method of blocking is with the palms directed toward the opponent.

cessfully is applying strong *seme* to begin with. If you wait passively for *men* to come so that you can counterattack, you will end up pulling your hands in. If you train with a mind to apply pressure on your opponent and coerce them into attacking, you will gradually get the knack of making them strike *men*.

I have seen many children perform magnificently at national tournaments for primary or junior high school, only to see them peter out at high school and university level. One of the main reasons for this fall from grace is that they spend too much time waiting passively for their opponent to make a move. Opponents often attack randomly at kid's level, so waiting to strike works for the stronger child. Once at high school or college age, opponents don't strike when they want them to. They have their own agenda, and being intent on waiting for the opponent to make a move will go nowhere. Predictably, the student becomes impatient at waiting, and makes a random attack only to be picked off. Then, unable to win like he could in his glory days, he ends up flogging a dead horse with his old habits of waiting. Even if he is advised that "waiting kendo" will never work, he finds it harder to break free because he has experienced the sweet taste of success with that style before. The only way to continue and enjoy kendo as you get older is to learn how to apply *seme*. It's not to wait and counter, but to create and counter.

This is the hand movement and position for receiving the men strike with the "opposite shinogi". Turn the wrists enough to reveal the top of the hands. This will enable a potent return strike to dō.

花ひらけ 地道な努力 積みかさね

Hana hirake Jimichi na doryoku Tsumikasane

To blossom / Is steady effort / Accumulation

Orikasa-san's Impressions

"I always had an aversion to kaeshi-dō as a technique. I hardly ever used it, even in keiko. After being taught a few pointers by Hatano-sensei, I feel I have a better understanding of what it is to strike dō with an adequate swing, as opposed to weak strikes that just touch the target. The problem is that where I train at Musashi Murayama city, most of my opponents are 6-dan and 7-dan teachers, so I never have the leeway to try kaeshi-dō out! So, a group of us with lower grades take time out at the end of training to practise kihon together. As we did kaeshi-dō over and over, the importance of maintaining a suitable amount of distance between you and the opponent became abundantly clear."

Orikasa Tamaoki (Assistant)

41 years-of-age. 3-dan. Studied kendo until his final year of high school but stopped after that. Orikasa restarted kendo after a 20-year hiatus. He is a primary school teacher and practises kendo twice a week.

This is Orikasa-san's kaeshi-dō after being instructed by Hatano-sensei. Receiving the men strike further out in front has given him more space to strike dō effectively.

REI

DAN

The Greater Meaning of Kendo

JI

CHI

Debana-waza

The timing for executing *debana-waza* is the moment one's opponent is 'thinking' of attacking, or the instant their hands start to move as the attack is initiated. This physical change that manifests on the verge of striking is called "*okori*". *Debana-waza* is meant to capture the *okori* and strike it down **before** it transforms into a technique.

(1) The Striking Opportunity (Debana) and Kamae

a. The striking opportunity for *debana-waza* is the instant the opponent decides to attack (psychological change). This might not yet be perceivable as an actual movement, but can be sensed or pre-empted. Feeling the opponent's **intention to attack** is described with terms such as "*nioi*" (smell) and "*kehai*" (sense). One can see physical changes in the opponent's expression and posture as they initiate an attack, but it is difficult to sense intent before it transforms into a physical movement. The following are clues to pre-empt an attack:
  i) The eyes become more intense.
  ii) There is a change in facial expression.
  iii) The grip and shoulders become tense.
  iv) The *kensen* and hands start to move.
  v) The hips lower slightly.
  vi) The right foot starts moving forwards.

Reidan-jichi Part 20
Waza Basics

By Prof. Ōya Minoru (Kendo Kyōshi 7-dan)
International Budo University

Translated by Alex Bennett

b. How should one's own *kamae* be poised to seize on changes in the opponent? A unification of mind, spirit and technique (*shin-ki-ryoku-itchi*) is the starting point, and absolutely crucial. This state must be maintained throughout the bout, and the initiative always taken while applying pressure in full spirits—i.e., not waiting passively for the opponent to move first and then responding. Moreover, when you do seize the *okori* and strike, it must be with full conviction (*sutemi*).

(2) Waza (*Debana-men* and *Debana-kote*)

a. *Debana-men*
Just as your opponent is about to attack, nip the movement of their body and hands in the bud by striking *men* before their technique forms.

b. *Debana-kote*
Just as your opponent is about to attack, nip the movement of their body and hands in the bud by striking *kote* before their technique forms.

Important Points
- If your body and *shinai* movement is not precise and strong, it will be nullified by the opponent's attack. You must be prepared to move forward resolutely.
- As both of you will be advancing, it is very easy to get too close for the point to count. To counter this problem, your striking must be sharp and timed perfectly—that is, before the opponent is in mid-flight, not during.

In the next issue, I will take a look at *hiki-waza*.

Kendo or:
How I Learned to Stop Worrying and Love the Olympics

By Michael Ishimatsu-Prime
Photos: Courtesy of All Japan Kendo Federation

There are no two words quite like "kendo" and "Olympic" that appear in the same sentence to get kendoka all riled-up. A case in point…

In August this year, KW's own Alex Bennett boarded a flight to Bangkok to represent the International Kendo Federation (FIK) at the AIMS (Alliance of Independent Members of SportAccord) conference. En route to a meeting, Alex made a Facebook post that read thus:

> *"In Thailand for a big sports meeting that could decide the fate of kendo in terms of its recognition by the IOC. Bit of pressure with a presentation the day after tomorrow... But all pretty exciting stuff."*

There was no mention of kendo being "included" in the Olympics, but still a few people decried kendo's imminent inclusion in the Olympic games and were fervent that kendo should have nothing to do with the IOC. As Alex pointed out, being in an alliance that is recognised by the IOC means just that; it is not the same as being an "Olympic sport".

So why is indirect recognition by the IOC important or even necessary? Simply, recognition by the IOC could mean legitimacy for kendo and its federations in the eyes of governments and national sporting bodies in the countries in which it is practised. This is not so much of an issue in countries like Japan and the U.S.A. whose federations are big and well-funded, but in nations where kendo is very minor, and has a small actively practising population, or is taking its first steps. Recognition could potentially be a boon for funding.

The kendo practitioners make their way into the Nippon Budokan arena

The kyudo koshiya-kumiyumi demonstration

A Polish respondent to Alex's post stated that in Poland, the government has pretty much deemed that the only sports worth practising are those that are Olympic, and as such, funding has been removed from those that are not. But more than funding, without IOC recognition in some form, international teams cannot be selected and national championships are unable to be held in Poland. This is why it is so important.

The FIK is a member of SportAccord (formerly GAISF—General Association of International Sporting Federations), the umbrella organisation that the representative bodies of Olympic and non-Olympic sports belong to. Due to a recent rift between SportAccord and the IOC, several member federations withdrew or threatened to do so from the former. The AIMS meeting in Bangkok was necessary for concerned international non-Olympic sports federations to meet and assess their relationship and recognition within the "Olympic Family".

To compete in the Olympic Games, membership in SportAccord or one of the other IOC-recognised groups is necessary. In 2006, the FIK applied to be a member of GAISF (as it was known at that time). This move was met by consternation by many practitioners who were wary of kendo "becoming an Olympic sport", particularly in light of the changes seen in judo since its inclusion in the Olympics. However, membership to GAISF/SportAccord was not sought with the intention of making kendo an Olympic sport, a point that was lost on many at first, including some in the FIK. Instead, inclusion was seen as a way to obstruct any attempts by rival organisations to represent kendo. Each sport is allowed only one international representative body. The Korea-based World Kumdo Association was formed in 2001 and was explicit in its wish to see kumdo/kendo as an Olympic sport, with rule changes being implemented if necessary.

Personally, I have no problem with kendo being an Olympic sport. The only caveat would be that it remains in its current format, i.e. no rule changes, no electronic scoring, etc. The argument on whether or not kendo should be included in the Olympics, however, is somewhat of a moot point: it already has, at least as a demonstration sport.

Tokyo hosted the 18th Olympiad from October 10-24, 1964, in a games that marked judo's inclusion for the first time as an official event. The newly constructed Nippon Budokan was home to the judo competition from October 20-23, but judo was not the first budo art on show at that Olympics. On October 15, five days before the start of the judo competition, a "Budo Demonstration" featuring sumo, kyudo, and kendo was also held at the Nippon Budokan.

After the opening ceremony at 10am, the day began with the morning session of the demonstrations. First was kyudo consisting of *hikime* (using a special arrow called a "*hikimeya*" that whistles when fired), *sharei* (ceremonial archery), and finally a demonstration by kyudoka aged between 71 to 82 to show the longevity of this art's practitioners. Sumo followed kyudo with a display of basic movements, *butsukari-geiko* (a type of exercise where one *rikishi* tries to push the other out of the ring), and a demonstration of the various techniques used in sumo.

The morning session was concluded by kendo with a performance of the Nihon Kendō Kata by none other than Hanshi 10-dan Saimura Gorō as *uchidachi* and Hanshi 10-dan Mochida Moriji as *shidachi*. They were followed by a jodo *enbu* by Hanshi Shimizu Takaji (*uchidachi*) and 40-year-old 5-dan and famed martial arts researcher, Donn Draeger as *shidachi*. Then there was iaido performed by six iaidoka of varying grades but led by 8-dan Danzaki Shichirō. Two Hanshi 9-dan sensei, Sonobe Shigehachi and Sonobe Asano, conducted a naginata *kata* demonstration before the session closed with kobudo (translated into the quaint English of "Ancient Chivalry Forms") of the Ono-ha Ittō-ryū performed by H8-dan Sasamori Junzō (author of *This is Kendo: The Art of Japanese Fencing* with Gordon Warner) and H8-dan Tsurumi Iwao, as *uchidachi* and *shidachi* respectively.

The afternoon sessions were one hour and forty minutes each, and opened with kyudo. It featured boys, girls and women's target shooting; a men's tournament to show the public how competitions are conducted; and finished with a *koshiya-kumiyumi*—an infantry demonstration by men in armour who apparently "hoot" as they fire. The sumo session featured 80 boys and men in bouts in the following categories: primary school boys, junior high school boys, senior high school boys, young men, and adults.

Another kendo performance concluded the budo demonstration. This started with a "basics" training session by primary and junior high school age boys. High school and university age boys—led by Takano Magojirō-sensei and Satō Sadao-sensei, both Hanshi 8-dan—demonstrated *kakari-geiko*.

These demonstrations of basic techniques and exercises were followed by two *shiai* components. First was a "Mixed Section" with two teams of seven practitioners that were divided into the following categories: elderly, kendo versus naginata (two), women's general, high school, junior high school and elementary school matches. The two competitors in the elderly section, Katō Shichizaemon-sensei and Nagano Mitsutaka-sensei, were both 83 and H8-dan, and were eventually promoted to 9-dan. The results of the "Mixed Section" are below.

After the conclusion of the "Mixed Section" there was a Tōzai Taikō (East vs. West) match with nine kendoka on each team. The East team won 3-2, and the results of the matches are below.

The West team's H8-dan Nakakura Kiyoshi and K7-dan Taniguchi Yasunori would both go on to become 9-dan. In fact, the latter was the 9-dan sensei that fought during the intermission of the 50th All Japan Kendo Championships.

Judging by the level of the kendo, jodo, iaido, and naginata sensei and participants that were chosen to represent their respective arts, it is clear that the All Japan Kendo Federation took this event seriously. And why not? With the world's sporting elite and many thousands of spectators descending on Tokyo at that time, the 1964 Olympics was obviously a great opportunity for Japan to showcase some of its budo arts. For many spectators it would have been their first exposure to them. An English and Japanese bilingual booklet was published for the event

Mixed Section Results			
	Red		White
Elderly	H8-dan Katō Shichizaemon (83)	*hikiwake*	H8- dan Nagano Mitsutaka (83)
Kendo vs. Naginata	(N) 7-dan Takahasi Hatsue (43)	*men dō*	(K) K7-dan Ōshima Kōtarō (47)
	(K) K7-dan Misono Isamu (39)	*sune sune*	(N) 7-dan Okuyama Sakae (42)
Women	3-dan Yaginuma Emiko (24)	*men dō men*	3-dan Nakamura Tamae (21)
HS Student	1-dan Takano Fumie (16)	*men*	2-dan Matsuno Kazue (17)
JHS Student	Takahashi Seiji (15)	*kote men dō*	Nakamura Yoshimitsu (14)
ES Student	Tonishi Masakatsu (11)	*kote hikiwake dō*	Ishida Takehiko (12)

Tōzai Taikō			
	East		West
Police Officer	H8-dan Tsurumi Iwao (57)	*dō kote dō*	H8-dan Nakakura Kiyoshi (54)
Mem. Parliament	K5-dan Usui Sōichi (62)	*kote hikiwake dō*	K7-dan Sonoda Sunao (50)
Company Director	K7-dan Saimura Tatsuo (54)	*hikiwake*	K7-dan Shimada Kiichirō (51)
Teacher	K7-dan Iho Kiyotsugu (44)	*hikiwake*	K7-dan Taniguchi Yasunori (43)
Police Officer	K7-dan Nakamura Tarō (42)	*hikiwake*	K7-dan Yano Tarō (41)
University Student	5-dan Ikeda Kenji (22)	*kote*	5-dan Taniuchi Mikiyoshi (21)
University Student	4-dan Kurasawa Tadashi (20)	*kote kote*	4-dan Tsuchiya Hiroaki (21)
HS Student	3-dan Shiraishi Masanori (17)	*men kote*	3-dan Fukumoto Hideo (18)
HS Student	3-dan Tamura Satoru (18)	*kote dō*	2-dan Masaki Yukio (17)

H10-dan Mochida Moriji (l) as shidachi and H10-dan Saimura Gorō (r) as uchidachi demonstrate the Nihon Kendo Kata

Hanshi Shimizu Takaji (uchidachi) and Donn Draeger (shidachi) demonstrate jodo

H9-dan Sonobe Shigehachi (l, uchidachi) and H9-dan Sonobe Asano (r, shidachi) demonstrate naginata

Junior High School competitors in the Mixed Section match

7-dan naginata practitioner Takahashi Hatsue takes on kendo K7-dan Ōshima Kōtarō in the Mixed Section

to help educate the public about the disciplines that they were about to see. This guide not only gave a run-down of the day's events, it also explained the historical, cultural, and technical aspects of each budo on display.

The kyudo section explains the features of modern kyudo, has photographs of the explanations of the eight fundamental movements, and details the characteristics of the demonstration events. The section on sumo is excellent, and is divided into "The History of Sumo", "The Sumo of Today", "How to Enjoy Seeing Sumo Matches", "The Rules of Sumo", and gives an outline of the demonstration. It also has photographs of some of the *kimarite*—decisive techniques.

The kendo section starts with two pictures of Saimura-sensei and Mochida-sensei performing the Nihon Kendo Kata, as well as a selection of photos that show the other arts mentioned above in the kendo demonstration. There is also a "History of Kendo" article, and photographs that indicate the target areas and basic striking movements. The kendo section ends with the following article:

Future Development of Kendo

"Kendo", one of the martial arts which originated from the use of a sword is apt to be misunderstood as a fighting and violent technique. With its special features different from Judo, technically, theoretically, and spiritually, it was only the Japanese who could fully understand the deep meanings of "Kendo", and it was rather difficult for "Kendo" to be internationally popular. Recently, however, an increasing interest has been shown by persons from abroad.

An officer of the United States Army said that "By watching Kendo he was able to understand the Japanese history and learn Japanese philosophy. Through the courteous solemn atmosphere a great spiritual depth could be felt which cannot be found in any other art, religion or sport." The characteristic features of this Japanese art have then gradually been recognised and understood by foreigners. [A] Kendo Federation has been established in the United States and interchange programs with Japan started. In 1955, students from Meiji University made a Kendo goodwill tour to the United States. In 1957 thirteen Kendo representatives from Universities of Japan toured along the Pacific coast of the United States.

Kendo Federations have been established in Brazil, South America and have been recognized as affiliate federations with the All-Japan Kendo Federation in 1958. [A] Kendo Association has been established in Taiwan (Republic of China) by [the] Physical Education Department of the government and interchange programs of Kendo athletes have been held.

Official interchange programs have not been held with South Korea but we understand that a Kendo organization has been established and is greatly encouraged.

This spring a British Kendo Association was established in London with General Francis Festing as President and Mr. R.M. Knutsen, to encourage the growth of "Kendo" in the United Kingdom. "Kendo" then, as will be seen, is becoming internationally known. We sincerely hope that the people throughout the world will become interested in the Japanese traditional Kendo, understand its spiritual background, and through it deepen the friendship among each other.

When this has been accomplished we can look forward to "Kendo" being included as one of the sports in the Olympic Games in the future.

The two 83-year-old H8-dan, Katō Shichizaemon and Nagano Mitsutaka compete in the elderly round of the Mixed Section.

Future 9-dan Taniguchi Yasunori (l) takes on fellow K7-dan Iho Kyotsugu in the Tōzai Taikō match.

The FIK was not inaugurated until 1970, six years after the Tokyo Olympics, but from this program it is clear to see that there was already dialogue and cooperation between Japan and other countries for kendo-related activities. What is particularly interesting about this article, however, is that it clearly states that the aim of the All Japan Kendo Federation at that time was for kendo to become an Olympic event. This sentiment clearly changed between 1964 and 2006 when the FIK's decision to seek IOC recognition was a means for kendo to not be included in the Olympics.

It is hard to tell if the Budo Demonstration was successful in attracting a new wave of practitioners or not. What cannot be denied is that the 1964 Olympic Games would have been a great vehicle to introduce and expose kendo, and also kyudo and sumo, to a foreign audience. According to the official booklet published for the demonstration:

> *It is our hope that this opportunity to view Japanese Chivalry Arts at these demonstrations will afford persons from abroad [an] insight into the real features of Kendo (swordsmanship), Kyudo (archery), and Sumo (wrestling) and we hope that this will in some measure lead to stimulating interest in these arts overseas.*

There is no reason why this could not be the case in 2020, when the Games of the XXXII Olympiad return to Tokyo. Kendo is clearly much better known and practised throughout the world—there are now 56 federations reg-

H8-dan Nakakura Kiyoshi (l) versus H8-dan Tsurumi Iwao (r) in the Taishō round of the Tōzai Taikō.

istered with the FIK compared to 17 in 1970—but IOC recognition could still prove to be beneficial financially for the smaller and less well-funded federations.

Recognition of the FIK in some capacity by the IOC is a no-brainer, but next time you are asked if kendo should be included in the Olympics as an official demonstration event, what would your answer be? Well, back then if it was good enough for Mochida Moriji-sensei and his contemporaries…

Kendo From Basics

By Kendo Kyōshi 8-dan Hirakawa Nobuo
Translated by Michael Ishimatsu-Prime

Hirakawa Nobuo-sensei's *Kendo From Basics* was originally published in 1993. It proved to be very popular and went through several printings in the original Japanese. Chinese and Korean language translations have also been made, and now, *Kendo World* has translated it into English and will publish it in 2016.

As the title of the book suggests, it starts with a discussion of the basics. This includes explanations of *shizentai*, *rei*, *kamae*, *ashi-sabaki*, and basic strikes and how to receive them. These are then used as the base for very detailed examinations of *uchi-otoshi-waza*, *harai-waza*, *tsubazeriai-waza*, *katsugi-waza*, *kaeshi-waza*, *nuki-waza*, *suriage-waza*, *osae-waza*, *maki-waza*, and *jōdan-waza*, in the Applied Techniques chapter.

The *Kendo World* team spent a few days in the summer and winter with Hirakawa-sensei at Noma Dojo in Tokyo retaking all the photos. Unlike the original Japanese edition, the *Kendo World* version will be full colour and also available in the Zinio ebook format. As a preview, here is a section from the Applied Techniques chapter.

Applied Techniques

Creating an opening with body movements

In kendo it is difficult to take a point if both competitors maintain perfectly straight *kamae*. The following is an explanation of how to use the body to cut across the opponent's centreline, or conversely, how to take the opponent's centreline to create a striking opportunity.

1. **Move forward to the diagonal right. When your opponent follows, immediately return to the original position and take the centre. With the opponent's centreline now controlled, strike centre-*men*, right-*kote*, or *tsuki* from the *ura* side.**

Important Points
- Without breaking *chudan*, stabilise the legs and move the body centred at the hips.
- Move forward to the diagonal right, and use the tip of the *shinai* with the feeling of executing a *tsuki* technique.
- Moving forward to the diagonal right can be done quickly or slowly, but the return should be done quickly in one breath, and as one movement.
- When moving forward to the diagonal right, the right foot is moved, leaving the left where it is. Then the right foot is quickly returned to its original position over the centreline.

Striking right-kote

Striking centre-men – forward, diagonal left

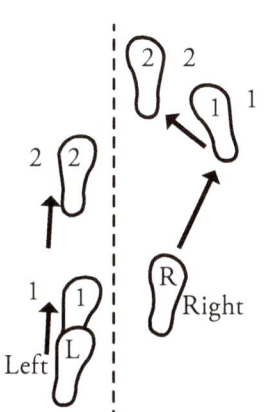

① *Footwork to strike right-kote*

Ura-tsuki

2. **Move forward to the diagonal left. When the opponent follows, immediately return to the original position over the centreline. With the opponent's centre taken, strike centre-*men* or do *omote-tsuki*.**

Important Points
- When moving forward to the diagonal left, it is important to keep the hips on the centreline and add pressure by moving as if about to execute an *omote-tsuki* or a strike to right-*kote*.
- Move the body forward to the diagonal left slowly, but move quickly when moving back to the original position.

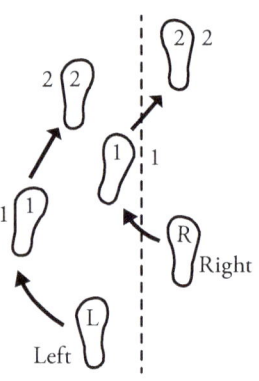

② *Footwork for moving forward diagonally left*

Striking right-kote

3. **Pressure the opponent's centre and move forward to the diagonal right. With the opponent's centre taken, strike centre-*men*, right or left *doh* or *omote-tsuki*.**

Important Points
- Pressure the opponent's centre in a small, sharp movement, and then immediately move quickly and slightly forward to the diagonal right to take the centreline.
- To prevent the upper body becoming twisted and leaning to the left, be sure to relax the arms, and move with the hips in the centre.

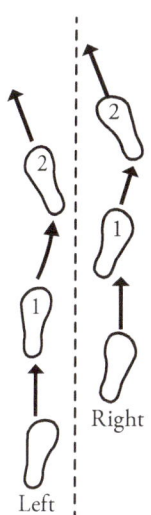

③ *Pressure the opponent's centre*

centre-men   *omote-tsuki*   *right-doh*

- The following three ways of movement should be learnt when striking left-*doh*.
  ① Step out with the right foot forward and move forward to the diagonal right.
  ② Step out with right foot and move forward to the diagonal left.
  ③ Step out with the left foot and move forward to the diagonal left.

Futhermore, when moving forward to the diagonal right, your opponent will often try to strike your *men* immediately. Bear this in mind, and practise dealing with this situation.

① *Step out with the right foot and move forward to the diagonal right*

② *Step out with the right foot forward and move forward to the diagonal left*

③ *Step out with the left foot and move forward to the diagonal left*

4. Apply pressure to the opponent's centre and move forward to the diagonal left. Controlling the centreline, strike *men*, right-*kote*, left or right *doh*, or *ura-tsuki*.

Attacking men

Attacking right-kote

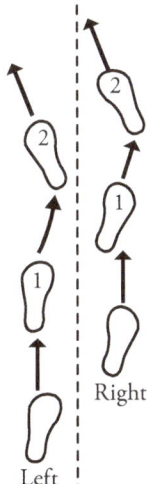

④ *Pressure the opponent's centre*

Attacking right-doh

Attacking right-doh with the left foot in front and the right following

5. **To create an opening, move the body left or right, forward or backward, three times in succession to break the opponent's *kamae* or take their centre-line.**
   ① Forward to the diagonal right (slow) – forward to the diagonal left (quick) – return to original position (quick)
   ② Forward to the diagonal right (slow) – back to the diagonal left (quick) – forward to the diagonal right (quick)
   ③ Back to the diagonal left (slow) – forward to the diagonal right (quick) – return to original position (quick)

Use movements like these to break the opponent's *kamae* or take their centreline, and then strike centre-*men*, left or right *men*, left or right *doh*, right-*kote* or *tsuki*.

Important Points
- Make the first movement slow and the second and third quick to break the opponent's *kamae*, take the centreline, and strike. Do not use only the hands. Utilise the hips as you apply pressure, and employ footwork with confidence to exert control over the opponent.
- Do not stop after just one strike. For example, strike right-*kote* and then *men*, *tsuki* and then *men*, or *men* and then *doh*. Practise using other techniques as well.

Attacking right-kote

Striking men continuously *Attacking right-doh*

6. Move forward and back to take the opponent's centreline and create an opening.

① Move forward (take the opponent's centre) – move back (move the tip of the *shinai* out from the centre and point towards the opponent's left chest area) – move forward (take the opponent's centre from above) – from the *omote* side strike centre-*men* or change to the *ura* side and strike right-*men*.

② Move forward (take the opponent's centre) – move back (the left foot should move slightly to the left when moving back, drop the tip of the *shinai* and change from the opponent's *omote* to *ura* side) – move forward (take the opponent's centre) – from the *ura* side strike centre-*men* or right-*kote*.

Important Points
- In the case of ①, while moving forward and backward, it is important to pay attention to *maai* while seizing your optimal *uchima* (the distance from where a strike can be made) and taking the centre.
- In the case of ②, use the tip of the *shinai* and then the feet when moving forward and back, moving the shinai tip up and down slightly as the direction is changed to take the opponent's centre and create an opening.
- In the same way as using the feet in *choyaku-suburi*, practise moving your centre of gravity quickly with the legs, maneuvering forward and back quickly making use of the recoil in the leg muscles, and striking from further away.

As in the case of ②, strike centre-men from the ura side.

Bujutsu Jargon Part 8

Reference guide covering various bujutsu-related terminology

Bruce Flanagan MA
Lecturer - Tokyo University of Science

52 守り刀 mamori-gatana

Knife or short sword (*tantō*) used on the battlefield to decapitate the corpses of fallen enemies or to commit suicide. Off the battlefield, a *mamori-gatana* might be thrust into a belt or concealed in clothing for self-defence. The term *mamori-gatana* appears in various historic texts dating back to the end of the Heian Period and was also written as 護り刀 and 御守刀 (*o-mamori-gatana*). An alternative name is *goshintō* (護身刀).

53 求道 kyūdō

The first character is *motomeru* (to seek/search) and the second character is *michi* (path). The term *kyūdō* refers to the pursuit of truth, or the pursuit of a state of consciousness or religious enlightenment, by following a 'path' as stipulated by a martial art, religion, cult, or other such system of beliefs, teachings, or life philosophy. The student/disciple/follower/philosopher is called a *kyūdō-sha* (求道者). In a Buddhist context, the character compound is read as *gudō* and designates following a Buddhist lifestyle with the aim of achieving enlightenment.

54 正眼 seigan

Middle fighting guard (*chūdan-no-kamae*) in Japanese swordsmanship in which the tip and length of the sword is aimed at the eyes of the opponent. Modern practitioners of sword arts often differentiate between *chūdan-no-kamae* and *seigan*, as variations of *chūdan* may have the blade tip aimed at the opponent's throat or chest. Historically however, *seigan* was simply the original name for *chūdan-no-kamae*. *Seigan* is a defensive yet threatening sword position and both two-handed (*ryōte-seigan*) and singlehanded (*katate-seigan*) versions exist. The term can also be written with the characters 青眼, 星眼, 清眼 and 晴眼.

55 一刀両断 ittō-ryōdan

Four character compound (*yoji-jukugo*) originally meaning to cut something completely in two with one swift and powerful cut. Yagyū Shinkage-ryū swordsmanship features a powerful vertical cut from a *jōdan* position referred to as *ittō-ryōdan* with the characters 一刀両段. In modern day usage, *ittō-ryōdan* means to use swift, decisive, and often drastic measures to solve a problem.

 # 56 十手 jitte

The baton/truncheon weapon carried and popularised by the security forces (*hori*) of the Edo Period. It was approximately 1 *shaku* and 5 *sun* (45cm) in length and was generally made of iron or brass. The *hori* employed the *jitte* in a non-lethal manner when subduing unarmed suspects or to trap the sword blade or weapons of armed suspects. A metal prong protruding from the shaft of the *jitte* above the handgrip allowed the wielder to block or ensnare bladed-weapons. A color-coded knotted-cord hanging from the pommel of the weapon was used to designate the rank of the *hori* officer. The weapon name could also be pronounced *jittei* and was also written 十挺 or 実手.

 # 57 竹刀 shinai

Bamboo training sword generally made of four slats of bamboo held together at the base by a leather grip and at the top by a leather tip. These two fixtures are joined by a cord and the slats are bound together with a leather tie. The exact origins of the *shinai* are unclear but inspiration may have come from the *shinai* (撓), a small marker-flag made of bamboo and cloth, the etymology of which is the verb *shinau* (撓う) or *shinaeru* (撓える), to bend without breaking. Accordingly, the word *shinai* referring to the bamboo sword was also pronounced *shinae* and could be written as 撓 or 橈. The characters 竹刀 were substituted later. Yagyū-ryū, among other arts, has a long history of training with the *fukuro-shinai* (袋竹刀), also known as the *hikihada-shinai* (蟇肌竹刀), a single piece of bamboo with the length cut and splayed into multiple thin strips and covered in a sheath-like cylindrical piece of leather. It is commonly thought that the *fukuro-shinai* of Yagyū-ryū was the first *shinai* ever developed.

 # 58 柔 yawara

The name for unarmed fighting techniques historically used on battlefields in Japan, however the term *yawara* also encompassed scenarios where one wields an inferior weapon to one's opponent, such as a knife against a sword. The term *yawara* uses the character for 'soft' and could also be written 柔ら, 軟ら, 和ら, and 和術, implying that suppleness and flexibility are important in using the body (i.e. *tai-jutsu*), as opposed to using a weapon to overcome one's opponent. *Yawara* included punches, thrusts, strikes, kicks, throws, locks, holds, strangles, and pressure point attacks, and formed the basis of many *jūjutsu* styles. Kanō Jigorō took techniques from *jūjutsu* to develop judo and removed dangerous techniques in order to make judo into a sport. Although judo finds its origins in *yawara*, the modern art and sport of judo, which features only grappling, throwing and ground wrestling techniques, now bears little in resemblance with its *yawara* roots.

Bibliography

- *Nichijō-go no naka no Budō Kotoba Gogen Jiten*, Katō H. (ed.) Nishimura R. (ed.), Tōkyōdō Shuppan Ltd., 1995.
- *Nihon Budō Jiten (Zusetsu)*, Sasama Y., Kashiwa-Shobō, 2003.
- *Kendō Wa-Ei Jiten*, Zen Nihon Kendō Renmei (ed.), Satō Inshokan Inc., 2000.
- *Kōjien (Daigohan)*, Iwanami Shoten, 2004.

BOOK REVIEW

THE BOOK OF SAMURAI
THE COLLECTED SCROLLS OF NATORI-RYU —BOOK ONE: FUNDAMENTAL TEACHINGS

By Antony Cummins, Yoshie Minami
Review by Jeff Broderick

(Hardcover, 414 pages, £25/$35, Watkins Publishing)

Natori Masazumi was a samurai tactician who served the branch of the Tokugawa clan that ruled the Kishu domain, current Wakayama prefecture. From 1654 until his retirement in 1685, he established the Natori-ryū school of warfare or *gungaku*, which was taught to the samurai of the domain. He also set about collecting teachings on a great variety of military subjects with the aim of preserving this knowledge before it was lost. Japan, after all, had become a land of peace under Tokugawa rule, and samurai were increasingly putting down swords and picking up brushes on their way to becoming bureaucrats and bean-counters. Natori's most famous work, the *Shōninki* (True Record of the Ninja) was a record of the *ninjutsu* teachings of his school, but this was just the tip of the iceberg; over many years he compiled a vast array of martial writings which have gone largely unnoticed—until now.

Englishman Antony Cummins and his translator, Yoshie Minami, have undertaken the enormous task of bringing this body of knowledge to light, and in the process, are attempting to breathe life back into the once-forgotten Natori-ryū. The present volume, which weighs in at a hefty 414 pages, is planned to be the first in a set of ten volumes. (Clearly, Natori was nothing if not industrious!) The book presents the first two scrolls of the school, outlining its basic teachings. The first scroll, "Heika Jōdan", lists 290 points that samurai should bear in mind during times of peace, such as how to make use of everyday equipment, things to remember when travelling, and advice on how to behave and conduct oneself in society. The second scroll, "Ippei Yōkō" (Important Points for the Independent Soldier), contains 29 chapters and many hundreds of points concerning the knowledge necessary for samurai on the field of battle.

Among these points are to be found many nuggets of wisdom which are as applicable today as they were 350 years ago. For example, from "Points to keep in mind about training":

[A] person may suddenly decide upon the study of an art themselves and afterwards have intense devotion, mentally and physically, day and night, for half of a year or even one or two years, but eventually he will become bored and give up. This situation will not produce a skilled person nor one who has mastered that path. It is like when trying to make a fire … if you suddenly speed up your drilling when you think the fire is about to ignite, the fire will in fact die and you will be exhausted … Likewise, when studying an art, start slowly and carefully and when the 'fire" ignites within, study with intensity. This is the path to excellence. (p.26)

Many of us training in the martial arts will be able to relate to this, and it is sound advice. Looking back upon my younger days, I also feel this passage, from "Meeting and greeting imbeciles", might have served me well:

If you are unaware of a person's stupidity then it cannot be helped, but if you are aware of it and still have dealings with this person, then you are also to be considered stupid. (p.49)

Alongside these and other gems, however, the book presents list after dizzying list of extremely specific details that will likely only be of interest to historians and anthropologists. Is there much desire to know, for example, about the various types of lucky and unlucky hair whorls on horses? About auspicious and inauspicious times of day and compass directions? The names for the many different kinds of war banners? Or the various, obscure ways to count groups of people, helmets, or armour? Perhaps most disturbingly, the book devotes a troubling amount of space to describing how to take enemy heads.

I would like to say at this point that I am not totally naive, and I understand the historical context in which samurai operated. They were professional soldiers, and cutting off the head of a fallen enemy was an important way for them to prove their valorous acts upon the battlefield. Reading this book, however, which includes sections on how to peel the face off an enemy head, made me keenly aware of the enormous gulf that exists between our time, and theirs.

On one hand, perhaps this very fact should be considered a virtue of the book: it rather quickly dispels any illusions we might harbour that the samurai were cherry-blossom admiring poets first, and reluctant warriors second. That aspect aside, the cold practicality of some of the teachings gave a taint to the sections that I found otherwise interesting. It was hard for me to take seriously any advice from a source who was so thoroughly superstitious as to view the coloration of some horses as ill-omened, and so cold-blooded as to detail how to strike the eyes of a decapitated head with a sword pommel so as to prevent them from goggling inappropriately before presentation to one's lord.

Cummins and Minami cannot be blamed for the content of the scrolls, of course. But a more immediate, practical problem with the book is its lack of organisation. However, this is due to the way the original scrolls were compiled and recorded; Natori seems to have written things down as they occurred to him. This randomness is also common to other books such as Hagakure, but because of this book's size and its lack of an index, it can at times be difficult to go back and find passages of interest. I hope that future volumes remedy this drawback by including a full index. On the plus side, the book is handsomely presented and the text is very readable. Rendering medieval Japanese into modern English—even modern Japanese for that matter—is not an easy task, but the translation in this volume is clear and readable.

Anthony Cummins and Yoshie Minami have begun a monumental undertaking with this project. They should be commended for bringing this information to the community of martial artists and historians who will find it of interest because, as mentioned above, it offers a detailed insight into aspects of the lives of samurai that usually do not get much attention. Part of me wonders, however, what role this information could possibly serve in our lives. Today, people who cut off heads are no longer viewed as chivalrous heroes, but rather as deplorable murderers living in a bygone age. The world has changed a great deal since the 17th century, and thank goodness for that.

Budo Finder Interview

Kendo World's Michael Ishimatsu-Prime speaks to Budo Finder's Djuro Stojanovic about their new martial arts community website.

What is Budo Finder and what is it for?

Budo Finder is a community marketplace for martial arts. It's a platform where users can promote their club or event, connect with others who are practising martial arts, or view a selection of martial arts equipment.

We want to bring a completely new experience, based on the latest technology, to the world of traditional martial arts. Technological innovation is taking place at a breath-taking pace, and there are now social networks, e-commerce sites, and online marketplaces widely available to the public. These new online technologies enable people to collaborate to create, share and publish information. We believe that there is a great opportunity for using new technology to promote martial arts and open new possibilities for connecting East and West, modern and traditional. We would like to help the martial arts community become closer and have a common place for sharing their experiences.

When did you get the idea for Budo Finder, and how long was it until it was up and running?

It was a process that took a while. We always thought that it would be great to have one place where you can connect with the people and get the latest information about clubs and events. So we started a pilot project a year ago just to check the idea, and had a great response, especially from the kendo community.

In May this year we realised that this could be a great opportunity to do something more than just a side project. We got the seed investment from the Eleven Accelerator Venture Fund and completely dedicated ourselves to developing the platform. In September we started with the full service, and now we are focused on growing our content and user base.

What does Budo Finder offer that other martial arts websites do not?

We are developing services around three focal points: Community; Dojos and Events; and Marketplace.

In the Community section, users can make their own profile, add contact details, achievements, rank, and a short biography. Once users update their profile, they can start

The Budo Finder Team. L-R: Igor Kojicic, Marko Andrijasevic, Blazo Crvenica, Djuro Stojanovic

communicating with others, or upload their own content, such as photos and videos. We are especially keen on promoting video material, user generated or from around the web, as one of the best ways to get users engaged.

In the Dojos and Events section, users can make a club or event page and enter listing details, contact information, schedule, photos, videos, and links to their webpage, Facebook and Twitter pages. This could be a great opportunity for club or event organisers who do not have enough time to maintain their own webpage. Here, you can put up your page in less than 10 minutes and easily promote it to the relevant audience.

We also wanted to tackle the issue of fragmented information about martial arts products. It is rather hard to get information about different products and suppliers in one place. In the Marketplace section, we want to present a selection of martial arts suppliers' offers, and simplify the process of choosing equipment for the practitioners. Even the smaller shop can present their offer, and we encourage everyone to contact us and share their offer with our community.

We believe that we are the only group who is providing all this information in one place, with a constant flow of news, videos and user generated content.

Why did you think that there was a need for Budo Finder?

We've been practising martial arts at the international level for more than 15 years, and we always had a need for a place like this. We have struggled to find information about clubs, events, and equipment suppliers for years. This is why we decided not to wait but to use our skills and build a platform where you can find all this information.

How has the reaction been so far?

We are really surprised how positively people reacted to our idea. In the last six months we experienced an exponential growth of users. We really want to be in touch with our user base, get to know them and their needs and expectations. Right now we are in the phase when we have many more users than we can handle. But we're doing our best to provide the best service to everyone.

Who is in the Budo Finder team? What arts do they practise?

We are a small team from Montenegro, Europe, and we believe that our real advantage is in the unique blend of martial arts knowledge and business development, and IT and design skills. Two of us have been practising kendo for years, and even participated at a couple of European and World Kendo Championships. Just this year, we had a great time at the World Kendo Championships in Tokyo, being part of the Montenegro National Team, and had all the fun of representing our country at the Nippon Budokan at the same time as promoting our company.

Thank you for introducing your new venture, and best of luck.

Thank you.

Belabouring Each Other Fiendishly

The Early Days of Kendo and Kenjutsu in America

By Maxime Chouinard

Hawaiian Gazette, May 29, 1894

The history of *kenjutsu* and kendo has been well documented in Japan, but outside of it, there has been very little research conducted. Many people are probably aware of the relatively recent history of kendo in their city or state, but kendo's history before World War II is either unclear or unknown. In this article, I will present some of my research conducted by surveying American newspapers at the turn of the twentieth century—the period when kendo and *kenjutsu* were first encountered in the United States. It is a story that goes farther than questions of sports and martial arts, but also unearths some interesting aspects of Japanese immigration and multicultural relations in America.

Let us first examine the context. Japanese swordsmanship appeared in the U.S.A. in around the late 1880s. Martial arts in Japan at that time were coming out of their darkest period in recent history. Following the Boshin civil war, the Satsuma rebellion, and the overall violence of 1860s Japan, many of its people were happy to turn the page and forget about martial arts which had been used in these events. For many it was time for Japan to look to Europe for inspiration to achieve proper "civilisation".

The Japanese elite were also eager to appear modern and civilised to Western eyes. By the late nineteenth century, most of Western Europe had profoundly changed its sports to less violent and more codified formats. Football, which had been at certain times an extremely violent sport, could now be played safely, and boxing was moving away from its bare knuckle tradition to include the mandatory wearing of gloves. Those which could not be changed were repressed, such as *savate*, which was for a time outlawed in France as the empress Eugenie was quite shocked by its violence. Other sports such as stick fighting and faction fights (mass brawls often involving the use of weapons) in Ireland were suppressed by authorities in favour of relatively tamer sports such as hurling.

When examining American newspapers, we can discern two main periods when Japanese fencing received the most attention, mainly the 1890s and early 1900s. So what was going on at that time?

During the 1880s, there was a growing sentiment in Japan that Western culture was undermining Japanese culture and that Japan's cultural heritage should be safeguarded. One such heritage was *bujutsu*, but in order for it to fit into the new unified Japan, *bujutsu* had to also be homogenised. Therefore, in 1895 the Dai-Nippon Butoku Kai was founded and its mission was to standardise martial arts and promote them along with the virtues of bushido and warrior culture. It is in this environment that *gekken* began to thrive.

Gekken was different from today's kendo mainly because of its rules. Grappling was allowed and one could score points by tripping and even removing the helmet of a downed opponent. It is also useful to note that various schools continued to exist until the late nineteenth century and that there was hardly one single way to

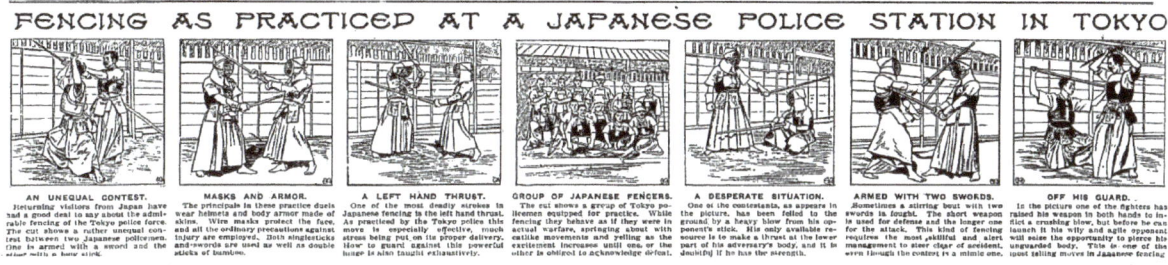

Gekken in the Tokyo police in 1906

practise Japanese fencing. This is why the term *gekken* is used interchangeably with *kenjutsu* in certain articles.

Outside of the purely cultural aspect, another reason was also behind this sudden interest in traditional fencing. The government was actively training potential soldiers to serve in future conflicts. Indeed, many instructors, some of them military veterans, were sent to the U.S.A. to open up *gekken* groups and shooting schools for expatriates in case they were called back to Japan to fight in its armies. (See the Shimbukan group in San Francisco below.)

As you will see, Japanese fencing was already being practised in New York long before the establishment of the Butokukai. Some Americans were introduced to *gekken* through trips to Japan and then invited instructors to come to America, and some instructors headed to the U.S.A. of their own volition in the hope of opening up fencing schools.

The attention of the media was especially taken around the Sino-Japanese (1894–1895) and the Russo-Japanese (1904–1905) wars. Before these conflicts, Japan was seen as a promising but rather weak military power. China and Russia had longer experience in modern warfare and also had superior resources at their disposal. It then came as quite a shock when Japan emerged victorious from these two conflicts. Something that was most peculiar to Western eyes were the feats accomplished by Japanese swordsmen who acquired quite a reputation, especially during the Russo-Japanese War.

At that time there seemed to have been two types of fencing in the Japanese military: a hybrid between the Franco-Prussian systems, which had been recently taught to Japanese officers mixed in with Japanese techniques; and *gekken*, which was more widely practised outside of the military. In fact, many soldiers would have had years of experience in *kenjutsu* or *gekken* before even joining the military, so many of them chose to use the *kyū-guntō*, a type of short katana with a two-handed Western grip, or even a traditional katana. Training soldiers in totally different types of fencing was probably seen as counterproductive. This is a subject which has unfortunately received very little attention in Japan.

Indeed, *gekken* was widely practised not only by the public and the military, but also by the police, and while it was not part of the official public school curriculum until 1913, Japanese swordsmanship was still taught in some schools on a voluntary basis.

The ability of Japanese swordsmen is often noted in many different American newspapers where reports of Japanese officers winning duels were noted. It seems the Japanese military—contrary to its opponents—still believed the sword to be a useful weapon of war, an idea that would continue until the end of World War II. This helped to shape the image of Japanese swordsmen in popular culture.

What follows is a list of cities throughout America where *gekken* was practised, or at least demonstrated, by the late nineteenth to the early twentieth centuries.

Cleveland

Surprisingly, it seems that Cleveland received one of the first demonstrations of Japanese fencing in 1889. It is not clear what the nature of the demonstration was, but a troupe of Japanese artists and acrobats was part of the Cleveland's Minstrels' show and demonstrated Japanese sword fencing along with other weapons. (*Plain Dealer*, July 19, 1889) This troupe did not deal in "blackface", as is commonly associated with minstrel groups, but rather presented acts of Venetian Renaissance and Greek and Egyptian Antiquity. This troupe held demonstrations all around the U.S., from Indiana to New York, until around 1895.

Gekken demonstration at the Sunrise Club

Honolulu

In May 1894, the Japanese man-of-war Takachiho stopped in Honolulu and invited reporters from the *Honolulu Advertiser* aboard their ship to witness a demonstration of fencing. (*Hawaiian Gazette*, May 29, 1894). One of the fencers posed for five minutes for the newspaper artist who drew the portrait above.

Two years later, the gazette reported on a club on Maunakea Street called "The Sunrise Singlestick Club" where *gekken* was being practised without an instructor (*Hawaiian Gazette*, January 28, 1896). Mr. Yamashita, a decorated army veteran, had been filling that position for the past six months it seems, but was recalled to Japan. The name of the club was explained by their location, just below a local Japanese newspaper called *The Sunrise*. Mr. Yajimai and Karikawa both held a demonstration for the reporters. The rules of this engagement were clear: only the head, wrist, sides and thrust to the throat were allowed. One visitor to the Sunrise Club even commented, correctly or not, that in the same year fencing in Hawaii had "reached a higher degree of development than in France". (*The Morning Times*, August 20, 1896).

Cohabitation with the locals sometimes brought interesting debates. In 1904, a minister from the Central Union Church had some Japanese parishioners who were practising nightly with wooden swords. Mr. Scudder complained not of the fighting or the shouting, but rather his problem was with the swords themselves. His argument was that, "Wooden swords are un-Christian, because Christ meant a steel sword." This was apparently from an interpretation of Matthew 10:34 ("Do not suppose that I have come to bring peace to the earth. I did not come to bring peace but a sword.") Efforts were made by the community to find steel swords, namely with Camp McKinsley and the National Guard. Both declined, as they were reportedly pro-Russian or neutral (referencing the Russo-Japanese War), so finding a private source of "tin swords" appeared to be complicated. (*The Independent*, April 21, 1904).

Duels also took place such as in 1898 when two Japanese men fought for a woman with katana with over 15 witnesses attending. The two of them, plus the man who tried to separate the pair, ended up in the hospital with critical injuries. (*The Pacific Commercial Advertiser*, June 3, 1898).

San Francisco

California was not far behind in experiencing Japanese martial arts. *The Morning Call*, probably one of the most prolific sources for martial arts articles at the turn of twentieth-century in America, published a story about a group of Japanese men practising a most extravagant sport, of which the shouts greatly shocked their neighbours. On Sundays, the 60 members of the Shobou Association met around the 300th block of O'Farrell Street to practise *gekken* under the supervision of Mr. S. Yamato, editor of the *San Francisco News*, along with K. Harada and K. Sawaki, both also instructors and editors to the journal. The practices were held right in front of a cavalry troop armoury, and the militiamen inside found the practice "impressive and violent". During their first practice, the soldiers actually ran out of their armoury expecting to have to quell a riot, but much to their surprise found the men fighting with bamboo staves. According to the reporter, three consecutive hits were needed to win a bout while the crowd judged as to the validity of the strike.

Another club was also very active in San Francisco as

Members of the Shobou Association

The Shimbukan, a gekken group with strong military ties

reported in the *San Francisco Call* on January 17, 1897. The Shimbukan met on Post Street for *gekken* sessions under the supervision of Sino-Japanese War veteran, Prof. Muto, who allegedly defeated seven or eight opponents at hand-to-hand combat during the war. The club, which counted about 200 members, was run with military efficiency, notably with the help of a bugler to call students to attention during practice. According to their president, Mr. Kurosawa, a sister club called the Giyudan was also founded to teach how to use firearms (bayonet fencing?). Kurosawa shed light on the sudden proliferation of *gekken* clubs around the U.S. According to him, the Japanese government sent instructors wherever there was a sizeable group of Japanese people and had them train so that if war was declared against Japan they could be called upon to serve in the army.

San Francisco at the time was a hub of criminal activity and violence, and friendly matches were not the only thing happening as far as Japanese swordsmanship was concerned: deadly duels were also being fought.

New York

New York City probably had one of the most successful Japanese fencing scenes. The Fencer's Club hosted a Ladies' Night on West 28th Street on February 27, 1893. (*New York Herald*, February 28, 1893). Among the bouts presented was "Japanese sticks" with Mr. Charles Tatham and Mr. W. Scott O'Connor. In November of the same year, a gala to honour their new instructor, Mr. Vauthier, was held. One of the guests present was Mark Twain. Along with the regular demonstrations was a *gekken* bout with Mr. Tatham and a certain Shilo Sacaze (Shiro Sakaze?). At the moment it is not clear where the two met or how Tatham and O'Connor even came to be introduced to *gekken*, but in the following years Tatham would teach Japanese fencing at New York's Fencer's Club, giving demonstrations to various groups. He had won silver and bronze medals in fencing at the 1904 Olympics. Mr. Sacaze is not mentioned in the following sources.

Tatham continued giving demonstrations, sometimes as far away as Philadelphia. (*Duluth News Tribune*, February 3, 1905). It is unclear at the moment for how long these lessons were given.

A husband and wife were also teaching *kenjutsu* in around 1897. Taneyoshi Kawakami and his wife Marumi both stayed in the U.S. for many years, and even taught *kenjutsu* at St. John's Military Academy and to General William Verbeck. (*New York World*, May 30, 1897).

In 1900 S. Akaeji and B. Makunaga, two Japanese sailors, arrived in New York City to teach *gekken* at a Japanese boarding house at 112 Cherry Street. (*New York Tribune*, August 12, 1900).

Gekken also caught the attention of rich tycoons visiting Japan or looking for a way to discipline their sons. One of them was Edward Henry Harriman, the president of the Union Pacific Railroad, who after two years in Japan decided to bring along with him a troupe of Japanese martial artists including the famous Mitsuyo Maeda (of Brazilian jiu-jitsu fame), Tsunejiro Tomita, and some fencers including Mr. Isogai and his pupil Mr. Mizutani, both of whom were from the Butokukai in Kyoto. (*Kansas City Star*, December 29, 1905). Interestingly, Mr. Isogai was also teaching Western fencing and naginata at the Butokukai, and it is possible that he taught and demonstrated the latter while staying in the U.S. They were joined by Kawasaki Tatewaki, the *gekken* and Jigen-ryū instructor at Tokyo College, who was passing through the U.S. on his way to England. There he wished to open a Japanese fencing school with "the support of men of wealth and influence". (*Omaha Daily Bee*, February 26th 1906). Whether or not this became a reality is still unknown.

Gekken even attracted some women such as Cornelia Bryce, the American suffragette who practised the sport which cultivated "strength and gracefulness". It seems that while *jiu-jitsu* was very popular with the boys,

Akaeji and Makunaga in New York City

Tatewaki Kawasaki and students

Cornelia Bryce Pinchot (dressed in black), suffragette and labour movement leader in 1933.

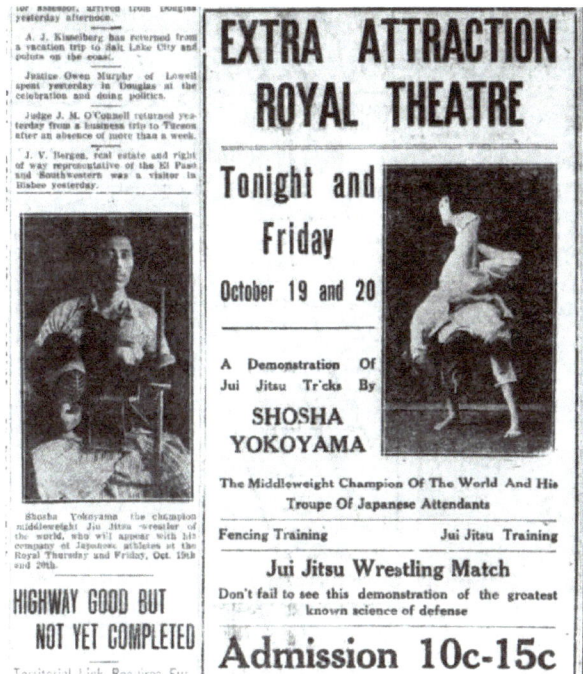

The Royal Theatre is still standing in Bisbee, although it is unclear what its current function is at the moment.

women preferred swordsmanship. (*Duluth News Tribune*, February 3, 1905).

Others found more practical applications for *gekken*, for example Rosa Matto, who coming back from an evening practice in Brooklyn with a friend, was assaulted by five men trying to rob them. Matto had a live blade on him and used it to defend himself and send three of their attackers to the hospital. (*Denver Post*, May 4, 1897).

Bisbee

This small mining town in Arizona saw a travelling Japanese troupe pass through headed by Shosha Yokoyama, a famous Japanese wrestler of the time. His shows also featured *gekken* demonstrations, as publicised in the advertisement above. (*Bisbee Daily Review*, October 19, 1911).

Boston

Interest in Japanese fencing in America seemed to mostly follow Japan's military successes, and after Japanese victories in the Russo-Japanese War, a renewal of interest in Japanese martial arts happened once more in the U.S. To commemorate the victory of admiral Togo, many Japanese groups around the country organised festivities, including both *gekken* and *kenbu*. (*Sunday Herald*, June 4, 1905). Due to the nature of this demonstration, it seems very plausible that a club existed in the area.

Kenbu is a traditional form of dance in Japan which is normally done with a katana and a fan. It has roots in the Heian period, but its modern version was mostly a product of the Meiji period (1868–1912) when former samurai were looking for a way to make a living in modern Japan by utilising their fencing skills.

The following year another demonstration was organised, this time to aid sufferers of the famine which was afflicting Japan. *Kenbu* was presented by Mr. Koyama and *kenjutsu* by Mr. Yamada. (*Boston Herald*, March 28, 1906).

Seattle

In 1912, a demonstration was organised at Seattle's armoury by the Seattle Press Club. *Gekken* and *jiu-jitsu* were demonstrated along with English boxing. Mr. Kikwaku and Iwaoka fought in *gekken*. (*Seattle Daily Times*, January 27, 1912). Again in 1916 the Seattle Federation of Musical Clubs organised an evening of music, but also with a demonstration of *jiu-jitsu* and *gekken* by Mr. Kasegawa and Mr. Manabe. (*Seattle Sunday Times*, July 16, 1916).

Los Angeles

Demonstrations were held around the Los Angeles area, namely in Tropico (now part of Glendale) in 1905 to commemorate Togo's victory in the Russo-Japanese War. (*Los Angeles Herald*, June 4, 1905). In 1909, a demonstration of Japanese fencing was held by students of the Los Angeles High School Gymnasium. Considering that *gekken* was presented without any fanfare alongside gymnastics, wrestling pyramids and tumbling, it is quite possible that it was practised at the gymnasium along with

Gekken in Boston

"Kembu" or Sword Dance.

other disciplines. (*Los Angeles Herald*, January 21, 1909).

A sword duel was also fought between two skilful women. Due to the timely intervention of a policeman, neither of the women died, but they were both slashed all over their upper bodies. (*Philadelphia Inquirer*, March 22, 1889).

Annapolis

On the recommendation of Theodore Roosevelt, the Annapolis Naval Academy decided to teach *jiu-jitsu* (judo) and *gekken* to its recruits in 1904. While the *jiu-jitsu* experiment did not last very long (barely a year), it is unclear if the fencing was also cancelled at the same time.

Others

Exhibitions were also given by Japanese groups in Portland Oregon in 1905 (*The Havre Herald*, August 25, 1905) and Salt Lake City in 1906. (*Salt Lake Tribune*, August 9, 1906).

Conclusion

At this moment in time it is still unclear what happened to most of the dojo and their respective instructors. Of course, by the 1920s kendo was already being reformed, which probably changed the practice of many clubs abroad. World War II also put a halt to the development of kendo due to the establishment of the infamous Japanese internment camps. I hope that this article will develop an interest in discovering more local history on Japanese martial arts abroad. With the development of online databases it is now simpler than ever to research. Also, why not ask the older kendoka at your club? They might know more than you think. Through these efforts we might be able to connect the early history of kendo and *kenjutsu* in America—and elsewhere—with contemporary practice.

Acknowledgement

Thank you to George McCall for corrections and pointers, and to Ben Miller for finding some additional sources.

Dojo Files: Wakakoma Kenshikai

Club Motto: *Bunbu-ryōdō* (Both martial and literary ways)

Year Established: April 2004

Venue: Vrije Universiteit Brussel (VUB), Brussels, Belgium

Number of Members:
Approx. 15 adults and 40 juniors and kids

Weekly Practice Times:
Wednesday, 19:00–21:00   Saturday, 16:00–18:00

Classes on Offer:
The purpose of Wakakoma Kenshikai is to offer kendo practice to children and youth.

Instructors:
Yoshinobu Kurogi (R7-dan, Chief & Founder)
Serge Hendrickx (K7-dan, Founder)
Daniel Delepiere (R7-dan, All Belgium Kendo Federation President)
Terue Matsui (5-dan)
Stephane Klugkist (5-dan)
Yusuke Nakamura (4-dan)

Club Social Media:
Website: www.wakakoma.be
Facebook: https://www.facebook.com/groups/89472794526/

Typical Training Menu:
Dojo cleaning
Warming up and *suburi*
Kirikaeshi and *uchikomi*
Kihon
Jigeiko and *kakari-geiko*
Nihon Kendo Kata during Wednesday training for approx. 1 hour

Club Mission:
We believe that the dojo is a place where both mind and body are trained. Through the practice of the traditional Japanese martial art of kendo, our aim is to develop future generations of children into good members of society. We therefore founded the Brussels Junior Kendo Club, or "Wakakoma Kenshikai", to accomplish this.

We hope that the children at this club will strive to understand and apply the following three principles learned during practice when they venture out into the world themselves in the future.

1. Understand and apply "*rei*" (manners) clearly.
2. Develop a tenacious mind and a considerate heart.
3. Learn our philosophy and transmit it to younger generations.

The concept of "*ken-en*" (relations through kendo) develops through the different relationships at our dojo, i.e. teachers and students, friends and acquaintances. At Wakakoma Kenshikai, it is also important that we promote and develop international exchanges between people of different nationalities.

The name "Wakakoma Kenshikai" was given to our dojo by K8-dan Hirakawa Nobuo-sensei, who has made great efforts toward the development of the All Belgium Kendo Federation. The meaning behind our club name is, "A place where children can learn kendo and have fun like young horses."

Samurai Green Tea

J-Concepts' Samurai Green Tea

ADVERTISEMENT

Traditional Green Tea from Makinohara City, Shizuoka Prefecture, Japan

The Samurai Green Tea Fundraising System

No matter how much we love kendo, the costs involved in it can at times put a strain on even the deepest of wallets. Buying a quality set of *bōgu* can require a big financial commitment, and we've all spent good money on a *shinai* only for it to break after a few training sessions. An even greater expense are the costs involved in travelling to major competitions.

With the exception of kendoka from the major kendo countries such as Japan, Korea and the U.S., many competitors receive little or no financial support from their federation and will have to largely pay their own way to compete in major competitions like the WKC. In order to help meet the costs of travel, some competitors or federations will undertake activities like sponsored *suburi-athons*. It is also difficult for small clubs and federations to purchase the equipment necessary to carry out their activities. With these issues in mind, J-Concepts and Kendo World have collaborated to bring you the Samurai Green Tea Fundraising System to help you raise money for your club, federation or competition travel expenses.

So what exactly is the Samurai Green Tea Fundraising System and how can it help you?

First, Samurai Green Tea comes from Makinohara City in Shizuoka prefecture. This is the heart of Japan's "tea country", and is an area synonymous with the finest green tea. Strongly linked to kendo, this tea actually comes from plantations founded by samurai-come-tea grower, Chūjō Kageaki, whose fascinating story is in the following pages. One canister of Samurai Green Tea contains 20 freshly-packed teabags that can be used to make hot or cold tea. You would order a

Seito Kenyukai Original Label

minimum of one pack of 24 canisters of Samurai Green Tea for $312, which includes postage to anywhere in the world. This works out to be $13 per canister. Next, sell them at the RRP of $19.95, and the profit you make can then go towards paying for travelling expenses, new club *bōgu*, or whatever it is that you need to raise money for.

A unique feature of this product is that you are able to personalise it. Create your own label from scratch or use one of our templates. Once you have placed an order and submitted the label artwork, the tea will be picked and packed, and then labels will be affixed to the canisters. You will receive your totally original canisters of Samurai Green Tea 10–20 days later.

---

1. Contact Graham, your tea and fundraising consultant, at tea@kendo-world.com to see how Samurai Green Tea can help you realise your goal.

2. Design your own label to the required size.
2. Choose one of the many templates and decide what text or photos to use.

3. Submit the label data with your order* and make payment.
   * A minimum order is one carton (24 canisters of 20 tea-bags for $312 including postage to anywhere in the world).

4. Once payment is received, labels will be printed and affixed to canisters.

5. Your tea will then be freshly packed, off the tree not the shelf.

6. Once your product is ready it will be dispatched by international courier.

7. Your carton of customised canisters of tea will arrive 10 to 20 days after confirmation of order depending on your zone. (Delivery times to South America and Africa will take slightly longer.)

8. Sell at the RRP of $19.95 to make $166.80 per carton towards your goal!

9. Still need to raise more funds?

10. No. Buy more tea because it tastes great!
10. Yes. Then buy more tea!

Of course, Samurai Green Tea need not only be bought for fundraising. It can also be used as a commemorative gift to give to friends or family.

Members of Canterbury Kendo Club that were selected to represent New Zealand at the 16th WKC in Tokyo used the Samurai Green Tea Fundraising System to help finance their trip to Japan. Here's what they had to say about it:

"The Samurai Green Tea was a low cost and hugely beneficial aspect of our fund raising efforts to get to the 16th WKC. The option to customise the label made it simple to sell to club members, family and friends. Additionally, as it is green tea, people needed little convincing of its practical value in comparison to other fund raising items we were selling."—Blake Bennett

"Fundraising has always been a tricky one for the Kendo Club. Over the years and campaigns, inevitably the same friends and family get asked for money or labour at various sausage sizzles and suburi-athons etc. This time, it was really nice to be able to offer them something back for their support. Even better, something relevant to kendo with the custom label and link to Japanese culture, and really good tea, too. A great fundraising tool that we will certainly be using again."—David Wong

So, why not ease the financial burden on your club or federation and partake in the samurai legacy at the same time? If you are cold, Samurai Green Tea will warm you. If you are too hot, it will cool you. If you are depressed, it will cheer you. If you are excited, it will calm you. Each cup of Samurai Green Tea represents an imaginary voyage. It is liquid wisdom with all of the health benefits Japanese green tea is famous for. Samurai Green Tea is the real deal.

Samurai Green Tea is

- **100%** PRODUCED IN JAPAN
- **100%** FREE OF PRESERVATIVES OR ADDITIVES
- **100%** ORIGINAL
- **100%** READY FOR DOJO FUNDRAISING
- **100%** PERSONALISED TO USE AS A QUALITY GIFT FOR ANY OCCASION
- **100%** DELICIOUS AND HEALTHY

Contact Graham, your tea and fundraising consultant, at tea@kendo-world.com to see how he can help you raise money for your federation or club.

contact us **tea@kendo-world.com**   about   **http://www.j-conceptsjapan.com/samurai-tea/**

J-Concepts 1082-1 Ieyama Kawane-cho, Shimada-shi, Shizuoka, 428-0104 JAPAN Tel.: +81 (0)80-3689-5978

Movement and Stillness
MEIJI SHRINE KOBUDŌ DEMONSTRATIONS
November 3, 2015 By Jeff Broderick

Takeda-ryū *jingai-jūtsu* opens the ceremonies with the use of conch shell signalling trumpets. By blowing different patterns, commanders could convey various signals to their troops on the battlefield.

Two different groups representing Shintō Musō-ryū *jōjutsu* (4-foot staff) demonstrated. The first group in blue trains under Arai Hiroshi-sensei, while another group in white are students of Matsui Kenji-sensei.

Hōzōin-ryū *sōjutsu*, or spearmanship, is practised in Nara and makes use of a spear with short lateral "wings" to trap and control the opponent's spear.

Toyama-ryū *battōjutsu* (sword drawing) has an emphasis on practical techniques and *tameshigiri* (test cutting).

Araki-ryū is a comprehensive art (*sōgō-bujutsu*) which trains in a number of weapons. This is part of the school's *iai* curriculum, which includes the use of two swords at once. In fact, many of the arts demonstrated the concurrent use of two swords at this event.

Nen-ryū is one of the oldest extant sword schools in Japan, and it are thought to have been the first school to utilise protective equipment, including headgear and gauntlets, to protect their practitioners during training.

The next time you are suffering while doing *suburi*, give a thought to the members of Kashima Shinden Jikishin Kage-ryū, who use these enormous wooden logs for strength training.

Yagyū Shingan-ryū is one of only a few arts that train in full armour, or *yoroi*. Their techniques are designed to exploit weak points in the enemy's armour.

Takenouchi-ryū *jūjutsu* is one of the oldest styles of unarmed combat in Japan, dating back to the early 16th century.

Tatsumi-ryū is a *sōgō-bujutsu* from Chiba prefecture, where it was designated as an intangible cultural asset. The unique "locked grip", used to secure the sword when blocking an attack, is visible (right).

Sōsuishi-ryū is considered a style of *jūjutsu* although they have a full *iai* curriculum. Unlike most other schools, which shake or "flick" the blade, the *chiburui* (blood removal) is very practical—the blade is wiped between thumb and forefinger.

Sekiguchi-ryū *iai* is a very pragmatic style on one hand, but rather spectacular on the other. Many techniques contain a jump into the air and a change of footing, called "*tobichigai*".

One of the most revered martial arts in Japan, Tenshin Shōden Katori Shintō-ryū has been practised since the middle of the Muromachi period (early 15th century).

Owari Kan-ryū is often thought of as a school of spearmanship, but it actually incorporates a number of weapons. On the left, the practitioner wears gloves to enable the spear to slide through his hands. The Owari school teaches the use of a short metal tube used in the front hand, which enables the spear to slide freely, so no gloves are needed. The school also incorporates *kenjutsu* including two-sword techniques, and techniques with long swords (*ō-dachi*).

The famous and influential Ittō-ryū split off into a number of branches, or *ha*. This is Ono-ha Ittō-ryū, well-known for its use of *oni-gote* (protective gauntlets). These evolved into the *kote* used in modern kendo.

Along with Musō Shinden-ryū, Musō Jikiden Eishin-ryū is one of the most popular styles of *iai* practised around the world.

Tendo-ryū naginata is a very versatile style which actually incorporates a number of weapons. Here, a long staff represents the haft of a broken *naginata*.

Shindō Munen-ryū is famous because of the many strong swordsmen it produced, including a number of the elite Shinsengumi.

Yagyū Shinkage-ryū is well-known because of its famous practitioners, Yagyū Munetoshi and his son Munenori, and as being the sword style taught to the Tokugawa Shogun.

Shin Musō Hayashizaki-ryū was founded by Hayashizaki Jinsuke Shigenobu, the "father of *iai*". This developed into most of the schools which specialise in *iai* today.

Takeda-ryū *yabusame* (mounted archery) takes place every year in a separate area. The procession is marked by rigid adherence to etiquette and brilliant pageantry.

BOOK REVIEW

HELMETS AND STIRRUPS

A Review of Helmets of the Saotome School and Stirrups for the Samurai

By Orikasa Teruo, Luc Taelman, and Jo Anseeuw
Review by Michael Ishimatsu-Prime

KABUTO

There is probably not a more easily recognisable style of armour than the *yoroi* worn by the samurai of feudal Japan. Ornately decorated, *yoroi* were more akin to works of art than protection in the thick of battle. The influence of *yoroi* lives on in the *bōgu* that we wear in kendo today; but different from *men*, however, the *kabuto* (helmets) are decorated with ornate objects such as antlers, horns, or maedate, and even *kamon* (family crest). *Kabuto* are still used in Japan today by parents of young boys who display them in their houses in the period before and after the Kodomo-no-Hi (Children's Day) on May 5.

Published in 2010, *Helmets of the Saotome School* is a bilingual (Japanese and English) book that introduces some fine examples of helmets from the book's titular school. The founder of the school was Saotome Chikara, a vassal of Tagaya Shigetsuna, lord of Shimotsuma Castle in Hitachi. Tagaya's properties were confiscated in 1601 by Tokugawa Ieyasu, the first Tokugawa shogun. As a result, Saotome lost his stipend but remained in the area and as a *kabuto* maker.

Following the preface written by Orikasa Teruo is an explanation of the *kabuto* of the Saotome school which introduces some of their special characteristics. The next section is "Mechanical Analysis on the Construction of Suji-kabuto". *Suji-kabuto* are helmets that feature a double-shell construction with hollow areas between the layers and reinforced with ribs, a signature technique of Saotome *kabuto*. There is also further discussion on methods of reinforcement utilised on *suji-kabuto*, and simple line drawings to illustrate these points.

Helmets of the Saotome School
Hardback, colour, 136 pages
€78 +postage

http://www.saotomebook.com/

Stirrups for the Samurai
Hardback, colour, 80 pages
€58 +postage

Two-page spread showing a kabuto by Saotome Iechika

This hardback, coffee-table-sized edition presents some 38 works of the Saotome school from the private collections of Belgian Luc Taelman and Aymeric Antien of France. Printed on heavy glossy paper, the *kabuto* are divided into sections depending on the era in which they were made: Ietada, Ienari, Iechika, Ienaga, Ietsugu, Ieharu, Iehisa, Ienao and Iemori. Each *kabuto* is photographed from the front, rear, side, and above, as well as from an oblique angle together with the plate that shows the maker's name. The photography by Jo Anseeuw, a long-term Belgian resident of Japan and a kendoka, is absolutely stunning. Like Orikasa Teruo, who wrote the short essays in this book, Anseeuw is also a member of the Nihon Katchū Bugu Kenkyū Hōzon-kai (Japanese Armour Preservation Society) and a photographer who specialises in photographing Japanese armour. Anseeuw's photography brings to life each of the *kabuto* that can be seen in amazing detail. It is even possible to see each individual thread of cotton used to join the various sections together, in addition to the intricate lacquering and marks made by the hammer as the metal was worked.

Unfortunately, however, this book does have a big drawback, and that is the English text. It is abundantly clear that a great deal of time and effort was spent on the photography, design and layout of *Helmets of the Saotome School*, but this is undermined by the fact that the English is on occasion difficult to understand. At times I had to refer to the Japanese text in order to figure out the English. This may be a problem for readers who do not have any Japanese language skills. Even though the written sections account for only 12 of the 136 pages of this book, I hope that the English text will be updated if reprinted in the future. If your interest is just in seeing first-rate photographs of some exceptional samurai *kabuto*, this book will not be a disappointment.

Two-page spread showing Kanzesui ni hatō kingin-zōgan abumi

ABUMI

When one thinks of a samurai's armour and tools, the image that springs to mind will most likely be *kabuto*, or maybe the exquisitely decorated *dō*, *kote*, *sode* (flat, rectangular upper-arm protectors), and *kusazuri* (the *yoroi*'s equivalent of *tare*). Or, a sword's *tsuka*, *tsuba* or *saya*. Something that I had never considered, perhaps because they lack the wow-factor of the above-mentioned items, are *abumi* (stirrups). Aiming to remedy the fact that *abumi* are relatively unknown, the same team of Orikasa Teruo, Luc Taelman, and Jo Anseeuw behind *Helmets of the Saotome School*, collaborated once again for the bilingual (English and Japanese) *Stirrups for the Samurai* (2015).

Stirrups are usually shaped like an arch with a loop at the apex through which a strap is threaded to attach them to the saddle. The bottom edge of the stirrup is flat, and is the part on which the rider places his or her foot. *Abumi*, however, are completely different in design. Only a fraction of the sole of a rider's foot comes into contact with regular stirrups, but the base of an *abumi* is like a board on which the entire sole of the foot is placed. At the toe-end, the metal curves up and back about a third of a foot-length in a cup shape. From there, another piece of metal protrudes with a loop on the end which is used to attach them to the saddle.

Stirrups for the Samurai features 20 examples of *Kaga-zōgan-abumi* (stirrups with inlay from the Kaga fief) from the collection of Orikasa Teruo. Considering the craftsmanship involved in the production of *yoroi*, swords, and their component parts, it should come as no surprise that *abumi* are every bit as beautiful and skilfully made.

The surface of the *abumi* is decorated with inlay in a variety of patterns—many feature *kamon*, or scenes from nature such as bamboo leaves or other plants, animals, or geometric patterns.

Like the *kabuto* in *Helmets of the Saotome School*, the *abumi* are beautifully photographed in great detail from several angles by Jo Anseeuw, and each pair are presented over two or four pages. Accompanying text is by Orikasa Teruo. He explains the genealogy of the craftsmen responsible for their production, and their particular attributes. A great deal of technical language is used to describe the physical characteristics of the *abumi*, so to aid the reader, the authors have produced a glossary for each of the various parts. The *abumi* are divided into three sections that represent the three families that were responsible for production in Kaga fief: Kunimura/Murasawa, Katsugi/Kaneko, and Koichi/Katsuo

Thankfully, the English text in *Stirrups for the Samurai* was very readable. Not least because each pair of *abumi* has a far longer and more detailed description than the objects in the *kabuto* book. *Stirrups for the Samurai* is a hardback, coffee-table-sized book with 80 pages printed on heavy, glossy paper that really brings out the best of Jo Anseeuw's photography.

Orikasa Teruo, Luc Taelman, and Jo Anseeuw have done a great job in demonstrating the skill of the samurai craftsmen with *Helmets of the Saotome School* and *Stirrups for the Samurai*. Knowing the authors' connections to the Nihon Katchū Bugu Kenkyū Hōzon-kai, I hope that in the future they turn their attention to full sets of *yoroi* or other items that further showcase the skills of the feudal Japanese artisans.

Samurai Skills

By Antony Cummins

Part 1: What is Gungaku?

"*Gungaku*" consists of two ideograms; "*gun*" (軍) meaning "military" and "*gaku*" (学) meaning "to study". It was the duty of all samurai to be immersed in military ways. The lower-ranked samurai were required to know the arts of combat and techniques of war, while the elite studied tactics and command.

Understanding of the samurai often comes from the later period of peace, but the truth is that the samurai were a combat ready force for most of their history. For samurai, the study of *gungaku* was as important as that of hand-to-hand combat, and should be considered as the iron web that holds all of a samurai's skills together.

This series will investigate the strategies and ways of the Natori-ryū. The Natori-ryū is a samurai school of warfare founded during Japan's Warring States period. The Natori family originally focused on military tactics and medical aid, serving the famed warlord Takeda Shingen of Kōshū. After the defeat of the Takeda family in 1582, his well-respected vassals gave their allegiance to the future shogun, Tokugawa Ieyasu. At this point, the Natori family split into several branches, one of which settled in the province of Kishū. In 1654, Natori Sanjūrō Masazumi began his service under the Kishū-Tokugawa Clan and was to become Natori-ryū's most influential master. He expanded the school and collected dying samurai arts into an assembly of scrolls, and moulded his family traditions into one of the premier warfare schools of his time. The scrolls contain a full curriculum of *gungaku*—all that is needed to take a fledgling samurai from introduction to the level of general, including the hidden skills of the *shinobi* and espionage.

The Types of Samurai

There are three broad categories that a warrior would fit into:

1. *Gunpōsha* (軍法者)—one who knows all military ways
2. *Gunbaisha* (軍配者)—one who knows the esoteric ways of battle
3. *Gunsha* (軍者)—those who serve as soldiers

The following are extracts from the scroll *Heika Jodan* (c.1670) and outline the responsibilities of the three areas described above:

> **Gunpōsha**: A *gunpōsha* knows the foundation of morals. He has mastered the *Goji Nanakei Shidō no Hō* in full, and has a sublime understanding of all aspects of victory and defeat in every detail. Furthermore, he fully understands castles, ground plans, mandates concerning military gear, astrology and astronomy, topography, human affairs, and also the art of the *gunbai* (see below).

Gunbaisha: A *gunbaisha* had a full understanding of religious services; manners and customs; military rituals; prediction of the auspicious and inauspicious through divination of date, time, direction, and lunar mansion; and other factors based on the destructive and creative cycles [of yin-yang and the five elements], and meteorological considerations.

Gunsha: *Gunsha* were samurai engaged in military service.

The Goji Nanakei Shidō no Hō

The above quote mentions the *Goji Nanakei Shidō no Hō* as the foundation of military study, and its contents are also found in the Chinese classics. "Goji" (五事), the first part, are the five constant factors found in Sun Tzu:

- The Way
- Heaven
- Earth
- Command
- Laws

This is followed by "*nanakei*" (七計) which are the seven considerations:

- Which of the two sovereigns is imbued with moral law?
- Which of the two generals has the most ability?
- With whom lies the advantages derived from Heaven and Earth?
- On which side is discipline most rigorously enforced?
- Which army is stronger?
- On which side are officers and men more highly trained?
- In which army is there the greater constancy both in reward and punishment?

Finally there is "*shidō*" (四道), the four ways:

- *Jūhō* (flexible)
- *Jakuhō* (weak)
- *Gōhō* (rigid)
- *Kyōhō* (strong)

A trained samurai would understand their place and usage, as well as knowing when to be flexible, when strength is needed, or when submission is required. These latter four principles form the backbone of a warrior's response and actions.

From Gungaku to Gunjutsu

If *gungaku* is the web that holds all of the teachings of the samurai together, "*gunjutsu*" is the practical application. While *gungaku* is to *study* warfare, *gunjutsu* is the set of skills that bring it to life. The Chinese characters used to write "*gunjutsu*" consist of "*gun*" (軍) as in *gungaku*, again meaning "military", but this time the suffix is "*jutsu*" (術), which represents "technique" or "skill".

Gunjutsu includes strategies for night attacks, incendiary warfare, water crossing skills, horsemanship, aquatic warfare, camp construction, castle defence, knowledge of poisons, squad movements, combat strategy, torch construction and the use of fire signals, medicine, rations, and all manner of elements that will be used in a military campaign. A samurai had to be a fully trained warrior skilled in the techniques of war. Natori Masazumi breaks down the basic areas that all samurai should train in into eight categories:

Bugeisha no Shinajina no Koto
(武藝者之品々之事—The Types of Martial Arts)

Bugeisha serve through martial achievements, and convey their paths to other samurai. The following list displays the kinds of arts that samurai should train in:

- *Yumi* (弓—archery)
- *Uma* (馬—horsemanship)
- *Kenjutsu* (剱術—swordsmanship)
- *Sōjutsu* (鎗術—spearsmanship)
- *Gunjutsu* (軍術—the skills of war)
- *Yawara torite* (柔取手—wrestling and grappling)
- *Teppō* (鉄炮—marksmanship)
- *Suiren* (水練—aquatic training)

There are many other styles; however, they are offshoots of the above and branch off into unlimited possibilities. Study each of these skills under someone who is accomplished in that way.

The level of training a samurai undertook was tremendous. *Gunjutsu* was a full-time, life-consuming path that would take years of dedication to master. Those who study kendo now have an obligation to know about the history of samurai culture, and I hope that this series of articles will provide a window into some of their original teachings.

The teachings of Natori-ryū have been brought back to life through *The Book of Samurai* series. Book 1 is available now from Watkins Publishing.

Hagakure and the Spirit of Zanshin

by Alex Bennett

In my previous article, I introduced relevant martial art teachings from *Hagakure*, a classic treatise on bushido written in the early eighteenth century. *Hagakure* provides a fascinating window into the world of the samurai in Pax Tokugawa (1600–1868). This was an age in which glory earned in battle was a distant memory for most, but the importance of overcoming the fear of death, and accepting its imminence, remained a central concern in the samurai ethos. Even in peacetime, nurturing the psychological strength to come to grips with one's mortality remained interwoven in the theoretical fabric of the martial arts. *Hagakure* can provide us with many hints as to how the samurai dealt with this concern.

Last time, I discussed the idea of "*sutemi*"—literally to "discard one's body" as the mental and physical state of total commitment in giving something one's all, even to the extent of sacrificing one's life if need be. In this article, I would like to look at another important concept—"*zanshin*."

Although nobody fights with bows and arrows, swords or spears anymore, the traditional martial arts of Japan have survived to the present day as thriving international sports. There is something that sets them apart, however, from other sports. Budo arts abound with old sayings and tenets of wisdom that provide a framework for life. *Zanshin*, or "lingering heart" is perhaps one of the most profound.

In battle, successful execution of a technique meant someone was dead. In modern budo it amounts to scoring a point against one's opponent, or hitting the target. Nevertheless, landing that crucial blow is only half of the equation. The warrior was taught to never let his physical or psychological guard down, even after victory. He had to remain vigilant, calm and collected at all times, and somehow manage to subdue the intense emotional excitement and adrenalin surging through his veins after a life-or-death encounter. This was not only a matter of survival, but was also a sign of respect for the slain foe.

Equating the warrior's heart with a cup of water, when the attack was made with sacrificial commitment and total integration of body, soul and weapon, the enemy is doused with the contents, and the drips that remain in the cup are tantamount to *zanshin*. In a nutshell, *zanshin* is continued alertness, situational awareness, and emotional control, ready for whatever, whenever.

Of course, this was pertinent in battle; but even in the course of daily life, the same important ideal was touted as being an important part of the bushido canon. Such was the precarious nature of life in samurai society. For example, in *Hagakure* it states: "A man in service should never drop his guard at any time; he should always conduct himself with the same attentiveness as if he was in the presence of his lord, or in the public eye. It will

seem as though the retainer is always slack if he is spotted relaxing during a break from his duties. It is important to always be vigilant." (Book 1–No. 66)

The warrior's reputation in the community of honour often meant more than life itself. If his character was tarnished though some transgression, something that would seem incredibly trivial to our contemporary moral outlook, such as ineptitude, a harsh word of advice to one's lord, or using the privy out of desperation in a married woman's house (11–77), then death by *seppuku* was often the only way to clean the stain away from the name. That is why *Hagakure* advises, "You need nothing more than to maintain a pure mind, and stay vigilant as you execute your duties. Just live for each moment with single-minded purpose." (2–21) Single-minded purpose and vigilance amounts to *zanshin*—it also keeps you out of trouble.

Again, stressing the importance of constant watchfulness in the course of one's mundane activities, perhaps the following represents something everybody is guilty of from time to time, some more than others. "Conceit and haughtiness are perilous during times of good fortune. One must redouble efforts to maintain a sense of humility. Those who revel when times are good will wither in adversity." (1–174) We all want to ride a wave of good fortune, just watch out for the sharp rocks below.

Similarly, regrets are something we all try to avoid. This is attainable with a good dose of *zanshin*. "There is nothing worse than having regrets," *Hagakure* says. "All samurai should take care not to do anything they will repent later. People become elated when their luck is up, and not seeing ahead, they drop their guard and come unstuck when things take a turn for the worse. This is a cause for regret. Always remain alert, and keep your feet firmly planted on the ground, especially when things are good." (11–40) Prudent advice indeed. But, perhaps my favorite *Hagakure* teaching on this subject is the deliciously simple recommendation, "Be sure to secure even a broiled chicken." (11–42). This has practical value in terms of samurai combat training, and encapsulates the idea of *zanshin* in the martial arts we practise today. Never take your eyes off even the weakest, most downtrodden of foes.

Still, any such credo is limited in its value if not implemented in some way in life outside of the dojo. The philosophical and spiritual underpinnings which remain an important feature of martial arts such as kendo maintain a direct connection with the battlefields of old. The world of budo is a precious legacy left by samurai warriors who confronted their mortality every living moment, and practitioners can gain fantastic insights into the beauty of life, and how to live it to their fullest potential. *Hagakure* is replete with fascinating clues to help guide the kendoka in this way.

Competitiors watch the Japanese drum performance

"ON LOCATION"
The Continuing Story of Kendo Wa
By Charlie Kondek

By now, you will have probably heard all the stories, learned all the facts, and seen all the videos of the 16th World Kendo Championships, which were held in May, 2015, in Tokyo. But may we show you another view? One through the lens of an intrepid film crew and a lean kit consisting of a couple of Panasonic GH4 cameras as they capture footage to make a web-exclusive documentary of the event?

In the last issue of *Kendo World*, we informed readers about *Kendo Wa*, a documentary film being produced by members of the Canadian kendo community about the national team's experiences at the WKC. The title, *Kendo Wa*, among its many translations, can mean "team harmony", and the filmmakers, while setting out to tell the story of Team Canada's participation in the WKC, are also out to tell the story of the international kendo "team"—or the world kendo community—that converged in Tokyo.

Convergence was a theme for Simon Conlin (4-dan) and Kelvin Ip (3-dan), the nimble crew members that travelled from Toronto to Tokyo to capture footage, continuing the work they and others had begun in

Ontario filming interviews and action of various Team Canada members. For Conlin, himself a Canadian kenshi of British origins that has also practised in Japan, what converged was his passion for kendo; his interest in the history of Canadian kendo; his interest in international kendo and athletes competing at the highest level; his passion as a filmmaker, producer and creative director; his commitment for the project; and the serendipitous timing and opportunity to observe and capture the 16th WKC at the historic Nippon Budokan. "The venue was so inspiring. I don't drop the word 'awesome' very lightly but it really was quite spectacular," Conlin said. All of these things aligned, making it a momentous occasion for our community, and Conlin and Ip were there to capture as much of it as possible.

Though experienced, Conlin said he and Ip "felt like press *mudansha*" at the event, handling sophisticated but unfamiliar camera equipment (see above right) and filming in what was for both of them a new style. "A lot of it feels like short glimpses of a larger, more intense path," Conlin said. "But I guess that's quintessentially what a documentary is." Arriving in Tokyo, they interviewed on location some well-known instructors in the international kendo community, and past Team Canada players. These included H8-dan Tsumura Morito-sensei, and K8-dan Shigetaka Kamata-sensei, as well as some of the *shimpan*, including Shigeo Kimura-sensei and Geoff Salmon-sensei, both K7-dan. Also interviewed were former European champion Fabrizio Mandia, current European champion Stuart Gibson, and 2012 All Japan Kendo Champion Kiwada Daiki, all of whom helped convey the immensity and sense of build-up to the event. The *Kendo Wa* crew were also on hand in the press room assigned to members

The crew of Kendo Wa used 2 Panasonic GH4 Pro Photo Performance Cameras and 1 Panasonic LX100 camera

of the Japanese and international media, heightening further the feeling of being centre stage. "The whole event was very well organized, especially the media section," said Ip. "I was very impressed with the professionalism."

Soon enough it was time to walk the area surrounding the shiai-jō to capture the matches. "There was such a great energy in the Budokan, I noticed a lot of smiles, nods and hugs and people reconnected," Conlin said, describing the feeling of the event. "A bigger sense of global kendo community camaraderie than what I was trying to portray with just the Canadian story. Many of the players, past and present, have obviously formed strong international friendships over the years."

How much of what they filmed will make it into the final product, a series of web-based videos telling the story of the WKC, is subject to the extensive editing going on as of this writing, but what Conlin and Ip noticed as they were filming were the kinds of details that might be more appreciated by kenshi than conventional filmmakers. He said his eye and his lens were drawn to aspects hidden to most, such as the nervousness of the first-time participants and the confidence of the more experienced fencers—it

The Nippon Budokan press pit at the 16th WKC

Simon Conlin catching some of the action courtside

GB's Stuart Gibson and Geoff Salmon-sensei (GB), one of the 16th WKC shimpan, being interviewed for Kendo Wa

was evident they had all trained hard to get where they were. Also to the poker-faced but calm demeanour of the coaches, who worked to hide their hopes for their teams so they would preserve the appropriate decorum as well as provide the unwavering support their players might need, despite what must have been overwhelming pressure, and to the international *shimpan*, concentrating immensely on the task at hand, under their own set of pressures over the course of a long day.

Conlin and Ip saw the emotion of the teams, whether elated by success or crushed by disappointment, and dozens of other important, small details between the bigger, more attention-grabbing details of what was happening on and between the courts, subtle nuances like the way some press officers bowed each time they entered or exited the main floor or the press room, which on most days is a smaller side dojo within the Budokan. "You could quickly tell which members of the press were also kendoka," Conlin remarked. Said Ip, "One of the highlights for me personally was watching Canadian Kyrene Kim's (4-dan) performance against Korea in the women's individuals. She really embodied the team Canada spirit, and even though she lost the match, she displayed great spirit."

"Being on the floor you could really feel the *ki* and *kiai* of the players," Ip continued. "I watched Japan's captain, Uchimura, during the Men's Team final and moments before Jo (KOR) scored the final point you could see Uchimura close his eyes, shake his head and compose himself. This was one of the greatest moments in the 16WKC."

The camera didn't follow them everywhere, such as to the "history of kendo armour" symposium hosted by the All Japan Kendo Federation, or to the team practices at the Olympic village, or to the pubs and restaurants in the evenings. "Those conversations are always kept as my own personal collection of fond memories," Conlin said. And, the crew probably didn't get all the footage of everything they wanted. But this is the nature of a documentary film project. "I regret not taking the chance to speak with both Teramoto Shoji-sensei and Eiga Naoki-sensei," Conlin said. In the past, both have crossed swords with Canadian *nitō* player and current Team Canada Coach, Matthew Raymond-sensei, and both have also been featured in their own documentaries! "Eventually it became less about what I wanted to capture," Conlin recalled, "and more about being very agile, letting great moments just occur and flow naturally, then seizing the opportunity as it presented itself... much like in *shiai* or *jigeiko*, I suppose."

Regardless, being on location in Tokyo was a memorable chapter in what has been a community effort—an effort of coordination, fundraising and social sharing. The film crew carries with it "a very positive feeling of honour and gratitude for the unique opportunity," Conlin said. "It was a serendipitous kind of journey. It just felt like a fortuitous sequence of events and the timing was perfect, better than what was originally planned and conceived." At present the crew is back in Canada practising a different type of cutting... in the editing suite.

For more information, please visit www.KendoWa.com

shugyō (n.)
The process of rigorously training and polishing one's mind and body. See ***musha-shugyō***.

(AJKF, *Japanese-English Dictionary of Kendo*)

The Shugyō Mind: Part 1
By Alex Bennett

"Make an effort to improve things that can't be seen. Make an effort in places that can't be seen. Then, your efforts will be seen by all."

We all know that nothing can be gained without effort. The more you put into something, the more you'll get out of it. But what is genuine effort in the context of kendo? It may seem like a tremendous effort to drag yourself to the dojo after a hard day at work. Maybe it's just damned cold, and you would far rather be ensconced in front of the fire enjoying a cup of hot soup. As for early morning trainings… But no, kendo calls. Wow, what an effort! After all, nobody would really miss you if you took a day off. Would they?

I pretty much guarantee that all of us have debated the pros and cons of going to training on a given day. Mostly our conscience wins, and when it's all over, we are glad we 'made the effort'. But should going to training really be counted as making an effort? Nobody lauds the sun as it makes its daily trip traversing the sky. It just does. And kendo training… Well it just is. To get really good at kendo requires considerably more effort than just turning up. The act of training itself shouldn't really be counted, as it is the bare minimum.

What do you do before training, after training, and in between trainings? A simple example: an old kendo teacher once told me off for stretching in the dojo. "You should be warmed up and ready to go before you get here!" he admonished. Hard training finished, and there always seems to be a rush to get out of the dojo. Watch and see how many people take time to meticulously fold their *hakama* and *kendo-gi*. How many, after going home, cool down with 100 *suburi* outside? What about extracurricular training for the sake of kendo improvement? The gym, going for a walk, reading *Kendo World*… My point is that the more one consciously does outside the dojo, no matter how insignificant it may seem, the more it will show in the dojo.

I recall my high school days. There was a lad in my year group who was far from gifted at kendo. In fact, he was pretty uncoordinated and clumsy. Two weeks before the 2-dan examination, our instructor commented that only T-kun was ready, and he alone was going to pass. What a preposterous notion we all thought! He's the runt of the litter, and everybody else is so much better. We had to eat our words and quite a bit of humble pie. Indeed, T-kun was the only one who passed. Apparently, our sensei had seen T-Kun sneaking into the dojo early each morning before classes just to do *suburi*. Given the severity of trainings each afternoon, the rest of us would never have entertained the idea of doing any more than we needed.

A few years later, I was 'enjoying' my first experience at the infamous Kitamoto camp for foreigners, back in the days when it was two weeks long. That was the first time I met the Brazilian kenshi, Roberto Kishikawa, now residing in Hong Kong. While the rest of us were licking our wounds under the dormitory air conditioning, Roberto was still in the dojo checking his *kamae* in the mirror. I remember one of the Keishicho instructors commenting, "That boy's going places." Indeed, Kishikawa-sensei passed his 8-dan recently. I heard from one of the examiners afterwards that he was "by far the best on the floor". That's what *shugyō* is all about.

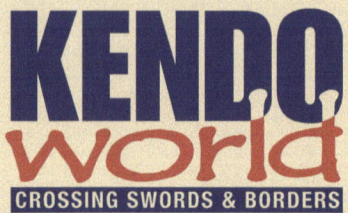

PUBLICATIONS
NEW RELEASE

A Truly British Samurai
The Exceptional Charles Boxer

Kendo World is proud to present its latest publication, "*A Truly British Samurai – The Exceptional Charles Boxer (1904-2000)* by Paul Budden. It is available now in Zinio digital format, and POD hardcopy.

Professional soldier, spy, linguist, traveller, international lover, prisoner of war and prolific chronicler of history: Much was written about Charles Boxer following his death in 2000, but few knew that in the early 20th century, he was one of the very first British practitioners of kendo.

A Truly British Samurai: The Exceptional Charles Boxer (1904-2000) gives a fascinating insight into the life of this extraordinary man, from his secondment to the Japanese army as a Language Officer, kendo training and life in Japan, time spent as a Japanese prisoner of war during World War II, academic career and private life. With contributions from family and friends, this book not only gives an account of Charles Boxer the man, but also of the kendo in pre-War Japan in which he was immersed.

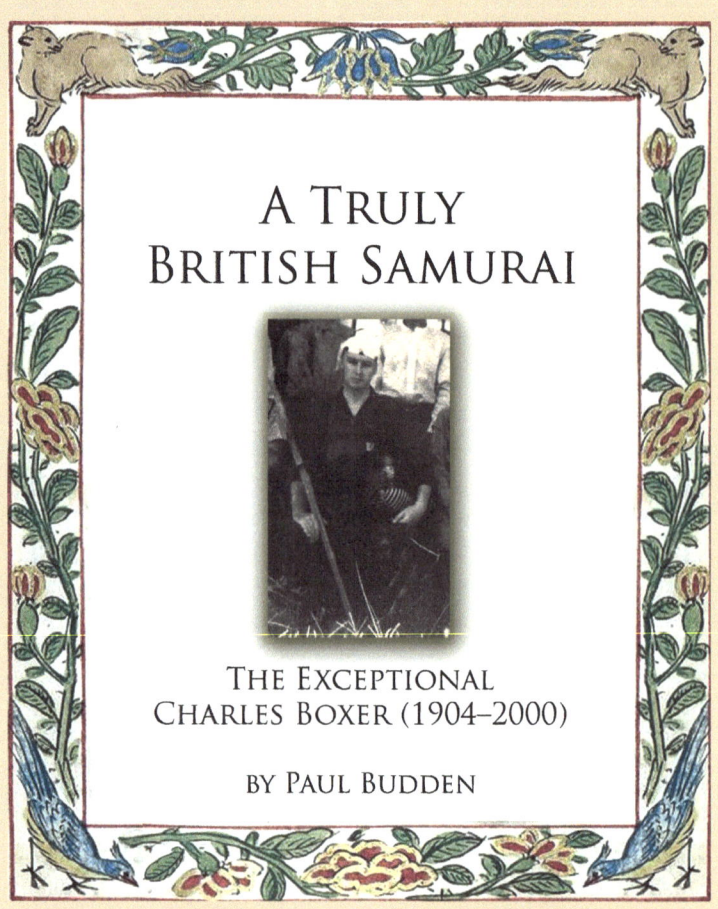

More info → www.kendo-world.com

Shinai Sagas: A Lonely Stone
By Charlie Kondek

And then we were all talking about Honda-sensei and his outrageous stories. This talk began at one end of the tables in the restaurant, one conversation among several. Apparently one of the people new to our area had an encounter and wondered how much of what was said was true. This was one of those nights at the college dojo, with Nygaard's and Mazurski's circle, so Honda himself was not present. But little by little the other people there, some ten or more, became aware of the topic, until by twos and threes we had all joined the discussion, leaning our elbows and forearms into the perspiration of beer mugs and chicken wings.

You may recall that story, told in Honda-sensei's way of speaking in English, not his first language, about the private kendo match that went on for years, the so-called "long *enchō*." Or maybe you heard the stories about Ogawara-sensei and his unusual training among supernatural folk. (Both revealed in earlier instalments of *Shinai Sagas*—Ed.) What was the story the newcomer related? It was "the lucky *shinai*". Some heads nodded. This was the one about the kenshi that received a mysterious blessing from a Chinatown crone—in some versions, apparently, a Taoist priest—gifting the kenshi with a *shinai* anointed to bring luck in competition. The owner of this *shinai* guarded it obsessively while he trained diligently for a tournament. He trained hard, but never with the lucky *shinai*—that he saved only for *suburi*, or for holding *kamae* in a mirror, lest he break it—and the kenshi counted the days to the tournament and imagined his victories day and night. The day of the tournament came and the expectant kenshi took his place at the appropriate *shiai-jō*, crowded by all the other fencers in his pool, putting on his *bōgu* while his lucky *shinai* leaned against the wall near him, and then grasping it gratefully, going off to battle. Sure enough, he had great success, winning match after match until he got all the way to the semi-final. At that point, with some time to wait, he took a break, sitting in *seiza* and removing his *men*. It was only then that he noticed over his shoulder his lucky *shinai*—still leaning against the wall where he'd left it.

In the clamour of the many participants of the *shiai-jō*, he'd grabbed the wrong one.

"So," Honda would say. "What do you think? It's not the *shinai* that was lucky. It's the fighter himself. Okay? This is the way to feel about a lucky *shinai*. You have the power. It is not the *shinai* or a trick."

All the time when telling his stories, we reckoned, Honda-sensei, a very modest-looking Japanese with smile lines in his face, glasses, and white dust powdering the folds of his hair, would watch you, try to observe how you were reacting to the story, how much you seemed willing to accept. And he seemed to adjust the details of the story, the cadence, the risks, to what he saw in the listeners' faces. In the re-telling of "the lucky *shinai*", several of us noted different details. One of us thought the *shinai* was not blessed but had achieved its power when the owner scored a very difficult *ippon*, or had a very good day in *jigeiko*. Someone else said it achieved its power because it was given by another, more successful competitor. And then the ending differed; some had heard the kenshi, upon learning of his mistake, promptly lost in the semi-finals; others that he realised his ability had come from assiduous training rather than superstition and went on to win the whole tournament. It seemed clear, examined that way, that some of Honda-sensei's stories changed with the telling, with the audience of the intended lesson.

Other times, it was not so clear. Had anyone heard "the fire revenge"? Many of Honda's stories took place in Canada, or Seattle, or California, or Japan, wherever the listener was least likely to be able to verify the details, and most of them took place in the recent past. "The fire revenge" was unusual in that it definitely took place in Japan and definitely before the modern era. Just how long ago was hard to say—it occurred at a time when there were still different "schools" of kendo (sometimes Honda called it "*kenjutsu*" or "*gekken*" in the telling), and each disciple of the various schools had to swear a blood oath to obey the rules of the school and keep its secrets. In this particular

A Lonely Stone

story, a swordsman of a certain school took an oath that prohibited him from ever using the school's teachings for revenge, as vengeance was not a virtue compatible with the school's ideals. Along with some blood oaths came a mystical punishment. In this case, the punishment for breaking the oath was described vaguely and poetically as "punishment by fire" or "an all-encompassing fire"; presumably, in the language of the mind, psychological or spiritual torment for the oath breaker.

As noted, English was not the first language of the storyteller, and so explaining concepts like "psychological torment" could be difficult, but also charming and tonal in its own way. In this case, some of us could remember Honda-sensei, sometimes—okay, often—aided by drink, telling us, "The rules of the school say, okay, you cannot use the sword for your own advantage, or, punishment. The punishment was like a fire. Like, your heart would be on fire, or your brain on fire. Like a torture. Aaaaah! Heart is breaking. When you take the *keppan*, it is like a magic spell. You don't know what's gonna happen."

The disciple learns wondrous swordplay, and develops great skill, not just in swordsmanship but in strategy and life. He begins to show promise as a man of ability and character. But then something happens that alters his course. He enters a *gekken* competition, and loses. This gnaws at him. It eats away at his growing and untamed pride. And so, determined to pay back this embarrassment, he redoubles his training efforts, working tirelessly to achieve not total swordsmanship but skill at *gekken*. His master sees right through this, but does nothing to stop him, apparently believing the student can only save—or damn—himself. Instead, after some time, the disciple, consumed by desire and smouldering with ambition, enters another tournament. His display is amazing, besting one opponent after another.

Each time he wins, he removes his *men* to drink a cup of cool tea, and finds his body temperature elevated, his skin hot to the touch. Surely, he thinks, it's just the heat of exertion. Yet the tea will not comfort him, his head when mopped by the *tenugui* burns as if fevered, to the point where steam rises from him. His master looks on saying nothing, only watches placidly (in Honda's English, "his face was like a stone, but, showing also some sadness. Like a lonely stone"); the master does not interfere.

Finally, the student engages in the last match—against the swordsman that dealt him his previous defeat! His body raging, it seems that waves of heat emanate from his *bōgu*

as he rises from *sonkyo* and presses his opponent's *kensen*. How his *shinai* must have radiated! How it trembled! Upon hearing the story one can only imagine the hapless opponent wilting from the onslaught. And yet, this is the swordsman that bested him once before, a student of a rival school. How calmly he assumes his own *kamae*. He is unperturbed! Perhaps the duel is like the trial between fire and water, the former shimmering, smoking; the latter tranquil as a pond, unrippled, waiting. When their swords crossed, did they hiss, create tendrils of steam? And then?

This story had two endings, we now agreed. In an instant, the match is over, but the first time Honda told it, the "water" swordsman overcame the "fire" swordsman, like a wave crashing over a rock, like water quenching flame, while the master looked on behind white beard and tired eyes. The match concluded, the hot swordsman, now as slick and humid as a jungle, bowed, and left the combat area, to retire behind a curtain where… they never found his body, only his *bōgu* and *shinai* in a heap of ashes. The consequence of breaking the oath.

In other tellings, however, the "fire" swordsman wins. He's got everything he wanted—victory by *shinai*. And… same result. Be careful what you wish for, what you swear to.

We paused, here, to wonder if most of Honda-sensei's stories had a moral. The moral of this one, it seemed, in either version, was never to devote yourself to the pursuit of tournament success or "superficial" kendo at the expense of "total" swordsmanship. The "lucky *shinai*" moral, too, was obvious, it seemed to us: there are no tricks, no shortcuts to kendo success, only hard work. In discussing "the fire revenge", some of us remembered a similar story about a neighbourhood tough guy (presumably a mobster) who had the bright idea to have his family crest tattooed on his right wrist—that way, no one would ever take his *kote*, because he would protect it so urgently. This worked so well he tattooed the chop on his head, then either side of his abdomen, and then finally his throat… His tournament success was legendary until that fateful day he received a *tsuki* from a neighbourhood policeman. And then? Same fate as "fire revenge," they "never found his body." Same theme as "lucky *shinai*", with a subtext of law and order woven in.

But not all Honda's stories had such moral lessons. Some, it seemed, were just intended to amuse, or to tantalise. Someone remembered "the longest *enchō*" being spun while at a banquet waiting interminably for a turn at the buffet. Someone else remembered a story about an eating contest between an American and a Japanese. (Where? Seattle? How long ago? "Oh, you don't know them.") Apparently, this was an attempt by some American kenshi to build national pride, because so many of them could never match the Japanese acumen at what is, after all, a Japanese art. In this story, which takes place at a "second dojo" at a Chinese buffet (always a buffet, never a barbecue…) the Japanese accepts the challenge—and the stakes; ethnic pride—and the best American eater squares off with the best Japanese eater. Here, details shifted depending on the telling, with the inventory of the consumed ranging from ten beers and cups of *shochu* to 25, three soups to seven, six plates to a dozen, dishes that included dumplings, noodles, pickles, cucumbers, cabbage, every kind of meat and fish, bones, marrow, cookies, cakes.

Honda could really spin this one in the right mood, and he usually finished it off by having both competitors and their entourage stumble out into the moonlit parking lot, weaving as if battered, the contest apparently a draw. Until… the Japanese vomits. Here, Honda-sensei would add copious details depending on the audience's tolerance for that kind of humour, but he'd always add that the sight and smell of the Japanese's vomit provoked the American to nausea… but he held it in. Heroically, he held it in, and he thanked the opponent, and they put him in the car to drive him home, and…

"They never found his body," someone joked, and we all laughed. No, in some tellings, the American projectile vomits out the window on the way home, majestically, but the result is the same, a symbolic American victory. This, when we thought about it, revealed another object of Honda's stories: to console.

Why did he tell these stories? What was it in the man's nature that compelled him to fabricate, to act them out? Honda-sensei was a dentist by trade. His practice was comprised mostly of members of the Japanese-American and Japanese expat community in the area. We imagined his creative impulses could hardly be restrained in this setting, and with such a captive audience, and in his own language! Can you imagine him, bent over a patient, fingers probing? "And what do you do? Sales? Oh, how interesting. You know, once in Japan I knew of a salesman so desperate to achieve his quarterly goal that he consulted a Shinto priest… and they never found his body, only his briefcase and prospectus in a pile of receipts…" Or, "And how is your son, Mrs. Tanaka? Studying hard, eh? You know, many years ago in Toronto I knew a family that was staying in the country on business and their son was struggling with his exams. To aid in his concentration, he wore a motorcycle helmet his father fashioned, wore it night and day… and when they finally opened the helmet, there was no one inside…"

It had grown late, and the talk was tapering off. Most of us began to pay our bills and peel away from the tables. In another part of the restaurant, the waiters were doing their side work in preparation for closing. A handful of us remained, including the newcomer that had asked about Honda in the first place. That's when Nygaard revealed to us that he had once heard that Honda in his youth had wanted to be a writer, but he had struggled with his parents over his choice of vocation, and eventually surrendered his artistic desire to pursue a more pragmatic profession. Besides, he calculated, he could always continue to write on his own time. But as the years continued and the pressure of school and then more school and internships continued to build, "his own time" dwindled into precious coin, now also spent on his work, his marriage, his children, his opportunities to study and work overseas.

And so where once novels shared space on the desk with textbooks, now records and invoices surrounded him. Where once he had kept journals full of short stories and novelettes between lecture notes and exam guides, now they sat in a drawer while he was occupied by X-rays and charts. The words he had once hoped to produce were shut away, so that fragments only escaped in the margins of his life, fables like "the kenshi's missing toe," "the blind *shinpan*," "the underwater *suburi* method," "the yen piece burned into the retina," "the kenshi that never washed his *keikogi*" and "the dojo that only appeared once a year and was populated by the ghosts of notable swordsmen". Honda's stories bled out of him. They'd never appear in print, but were written on that most fickle of materials, the human heart. Written and remembered, as well as could be remembered, by the people that knew him as physician, teacher, entertainer, interpreter, comforter.

Anyway, that's what Nygaard had heard. As with anything else involving Honda-sensei's stories, he didn't know what to believe. It was possible but not plausible, half invented, perhaps, to make a point. And what was the point? What was the lesson of Honda's murky life story?

In the parking lot, Nygaard ground a cigarette beneath his heel and walked off to his car.

Dojo Files

The Vietnam Kendo Clubs Association

By Tran Thanh Tung, VKCA General Secretary

The Vietnam Kendo Clubs Association (VKCA) was established as a non-profit association on January 19, 2014. Its purpose is to develop and foster kendo in Vietnam. Presently, the VKCA consists of 13 member clubs (see below) which have more than 400 active kendoka.

The VKCA is a newly established organisation and we are trying hard to learn about kendo and build up our managerial abilities. While we are being given great support and instruction from people throughout the world, we are at the stage where we are searching for the future direction of our organisation. In order to adopt constructive ideas and methods, we change our chairman every year, and we are also proactive in making efforts to reform our federation.

Since 2014, the VKCA has hosted the Vietnam Open Kendo Championships to provide an opportunity to cross swords and develop relationships with people throughout the world. The 1st Vietnam Open Kendo Championships were held in August 2014, in the modern and beautiful atmosphere of RMIT International University in Ho Chi Minh city. The 2nd Vietnam Open Kendo Championships were held in August 2015, at the An Lac Trang Eco Tourism Garden–a venue with an abundance of greenery and a wonderful jungle atmosphere. About 150 competitors from seven countries (Australia, Cambodia, China, Japan, Korea, Singapore and Vietnam) took part in the competition.

We are planning to hold this event every year, as well as various training courses. Everybody is welcome to attend these events. If you are interested in coming to Vietnam to practise kendo, please contact us at the following email address: thanhtung0508@gmail.com

Information about the VKCA

Date of Establishment: January 19, 2014

VKCA Members: approx. 400

Executive Members:
1: Shihan/Master Coach - Tsuchiya Makoto
2: General Secretary - Tran Thanh Tung
3: Secretary - Chu Manh Toan
4: 2015 Chairman - Long Hoang Ngo
5: 2015 Vice-Chairman - NguyenSy Hiep
6: Executive Committee - Phan Minh Tuan, Ki Oyo, Phan Duy Minh

Members of the Vietnam Kendo Clubs Association:

Hanoi City Area:
1: Hanoi Seikenkan Kendo Club
2: Hanoi Tsunami Kendo Club
3: Hanoi Centre Kendo Club
4: Hanoi Western Kendo Club
5: Ha Dong Seikenkan

Ho Chi Minh City Area:
6: Nitoukan Kendo Club
7: Kazeken Kendo Club
8: Toukai Kendo Club
9: Kenzenkan Kendo Club
10: RMIT SGS Kendo Club
11: Tinh Vo Kendo Club

Vinh City Area:
12: Vinh Seikenkan

Hai Phong City Area:
13: Hai Phong Seikenkan

Facebook:
https://www.facebook.com/vietnam.kendo.clubs.association

Website:
www.kendo-vkca.com

Musō Jikiden Eishin-ryū Riai
The Meaning of the Kata: Part 3

By Kim Taylor

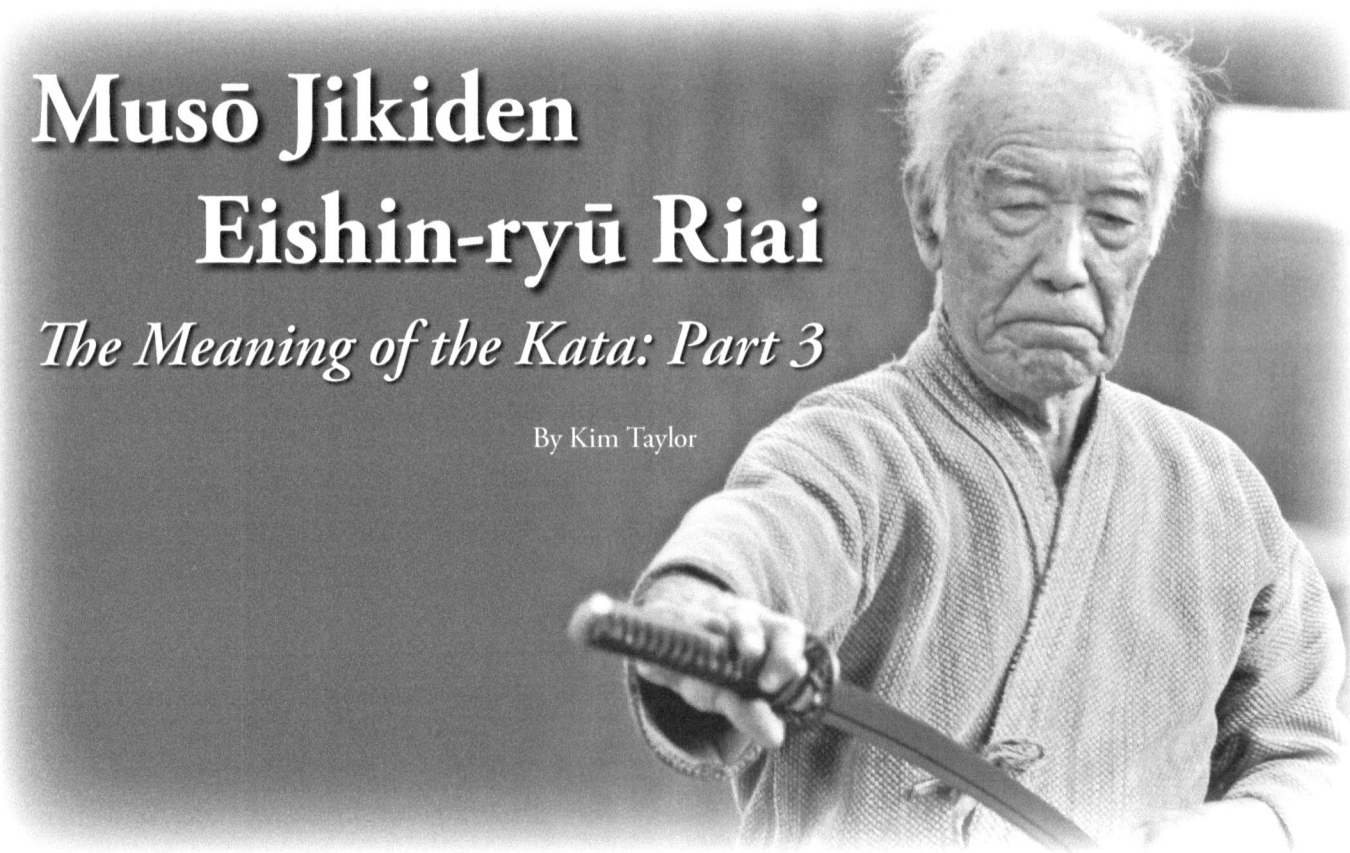

Introduction
This is Part 3 of a series of articles about the meaning behind the *kata* of the Musō Jikiden Eishin-ryū (MJER) and the organisation of those *kata* into their levels and order. I claim no special knowledge of the thoughts of Ōe Masamichi as I was not alive when he reorganised the school into its present order. I simply offer my thoughts on this from a background of 30 years of practice in this school and in some other Japanese sword arts. Please understand while you are reading this that this is one person's way of organising and understanding the material. You are encouraged to read this, compare it with what you have been taught and what you understand, and come to your own conclusions.

Set II: The Eishin-ryū
The first two articles in this series outlined Set I, the Ōmori-ryū, and described the *kata* fairly thoroughly. In order to avoid too much repetition, these articles will concentrate on the key points of each *kata*. Please refer back to the earlier articles in *Kendo World* 7.3 and 7.4 for details of the basics. The following articles will also assume some familiarity with Japanese sword terms.

The Eishin-ryū Basics
Once the student has mastered the basics in Ōmori-ryū, some things can be done at a slightly higher level of practice. For instance the final cut can be finished with the tip a fraction higher (with the *kissaki* at the same height as the *ha-machi*), and *nōtō*. can be done a bit shorter (with contact of the left hand at the *chūo* position, instead of the *tsubamoto*. This and a few other small points of style are optional or are adjusted as the student develops the ability to change them.

This set will review and expand what was learned in Ōmori-ryū. It will also introduce some *jūjutsu*—the method of dealing with an opponent who is inside one's normal *maai*. In fact, one of the distinguishing features of the Eishin-ryū is that it is performed against an opponent who is close. Related to this, the Eishin-ryū introduces the student to *tatehiza*, a starting position with one knee up. This position is much more versatile than *seiza*, not to mention more combative. It is very difficult to move backward from *seiza* but from *tatehiza* it is possible.

The *tatehiza* position is one that is much discussed and inspires much speculation. The most usual explanation I have heard over the years is that *tatehiza* is the method of sitting in armour. It may well be, but there is no indication that armour was ever worn by those practising iaido as we know it. While there was a great deal of warfare going on during the lifetime of Hayashizaki Jinsuke, the founder of the school, it was mostly during his younger days, and armour (at least shin guards) did not play much of a role in the age of the gun. By the time of the founder's death, almost 20 years of the Edo period had passed and very few people would still have been wearing armour. During the Edo period, armour would have been a relic of the past, and those wearing the sword would have been in an outfit similar to what we use in practice today. I just do not buy the armour explanation.

Tate-hiza

A much more likely reason for *iai* practice from *tatehiza* is that it was the formal sitting position before the *tatami* room appeared in the late Muromachi period. The usual and most comfortable way to sit would be *agura* (cross-legged), but this is not very formal or very easy to fight out of.

As the sets move from Ōmori-ryū to Eishin-ryū to Oku Iai, they are said to be in order from old to new, so *tatehiza* comes later than the standing techniques, with *seiza* as the most recent set and way of sitting.

Lore indicates that the seventh head, Hasegawa Hidenobu Eishin (the man after whom this set was named), was the first to put the sword into the belt and practise *iai* from that position. Again, the sword through the belt was a style that became popular in the late Muromachi period, so the time seems to fit, but I suspect the sword was worn in the belt from the beginning of *iai* as we know it today. After all, Hayashizaki Jinsuke lived from 1542–1621, while Eishin learned between 1713–1735, so there was not a lot of time between them for styles to change. Doubtless, the Eishin set was derived mostly from the techniques of Hayashizaki, and one can see similar forms in both Eishin-ryū and Oku Iai.

In this set there are three *kata* to the front, two each to the left, right and rear, and one last *kata* to the front making a total of ten.

Yoko Gumo

This is the most representative *kata* of the Musō Jikiden Eishin-ryū, containing the elements that are most commonly found in the three levels of practice. It is performed from *tatehiza*, is a horizontal draw/cut and then vertical cut, and finishes with *yoko chiburi*.

This *kata* is essentially a review of Ōmori-ryū Mae, but done from *tatehiza*. Here practitioners become instantly aware of the difficulties of the *tatehiza* position, not least of which for most Westerners, it hurts. It is sometimes years later that the benefits can start to be seen. To work well from *tatehiza*, it is important to understand that both legs must be used from the beginning of any movement; if one leg or the other is overloaded, we risk damaging our knees, especially if the practitioner is overweight.

Yoko Gumo - front

Yoko Gumo - side

Yoko Gumo

Yoko Gumo allows the student to become accustomed to *tatehiza* by performing a familiar *kata* (Mae) from the new starting position. In the Musō Jikiden Eishin-ryū (MJER) practitioners move forward as they draw, just as they do in Mae. In the Musō Shinden-ryū (MSR) the move is done backward to create space from an opponent who is close. MSR does this for the first three *kata* while MJER uses a forward, backward and "in place" pattern of movement. The idea is to practise variation where possible in the *kata* without forgetting that the overall meaning of the set is to deal with opponents who are inside one's ideal *maai*.

Tora no Issoku

This *kata* is a response to an attack to the shoulder, and then, as that target is removed, the knee, which is also eventually taken out of range. With this second *kata* of the set, the value of *tatehiza* over *seiza* can instantly be seen. To understand it "in your bones", try moving back out of range of this attack from *seiza*.

The block near the knee (*sune-gakoi* or shin guard) has been learned in the first set (Yae Gaki) so that knowledge is applied to the new *tatehiza* set.

The final vertical cut of this *kata* can be done in two ways: as the knee drops to the ground, similar to the step and cut of Yae Gaki before the knee strike; after the knee is dropped to the ground, as is done in the second part of Yae Gaki. Since the opponent is not lying on the ground when he attacks, it is in fact possible to cut him while still standing, but that is a poor strike with little power because it is at the end of the range of arm motion. To strike while dropping down into the cut gives more power, as does the strike done after touching the front knee to the ground. One traditional teaching that has been handed down is that we should cut a kneeling opponent from a kneeling position. During a *kata* when we have cut the opponent in a standing position, it is assumed that opponent has dropped to one knee, so we are invited to drop to our own knee to finish the cut. This has little to do with ideas of fairness or chivalry and much more to do with making effective cuts.

Ina Zuma

This is the third of the front-facing *kata*. The first *kata* presented a move forward into the opponent's attack while the second was a move back from the starting position, the first such move to have been made. This *kata* presents a move straight upward, or even a movement that changes from sitting on a knee and a foot to standing on two feet without moving the upper body at all. In short, the practitioner attacks into a descending overhead cut by shooting the left leg back to a standing position for stability, while drawing into the striking sword or arms. It takes tremendous leg strength to move into this position without raising the body at the same time, but the extra time gained by not lifting the head into the descending sword is an incentive to gain the necessary strength.

Ina Zuma is usually taught as a response to a standing attack, but it could just as well be a response to Nuki Uchi, the final *kata* of the first set.

First Three Kata and Review of Ōmori-ryū

By using the first three *kata* we can get a good review of Ōmori-ryū using a partner in practice. Tora no Issoku allows us to defend against the techniques Mae through to Yae Gaki. The horizontal attack from *seiza* is blocked by the first movement of Tora no Issoku, and then a target is presented for the vertical cut by holding the *bokutō* overhead. This exact *kata* will be encountered in the Tsumi Ai no Kurai set of partner practice where both partners start from *tatehiza*. Since the partner practices are a whole "other book", they will not be explained in detail here.

These three *kata* can be practised in a continuous manner: draw to the first cut then drop the arm to the side for a horizontal *nōtō*. Stay on the toes while pulling the right foot back and then draw immediately into the next position for a horizontal, downward, upward draw practice.

Tora no Issoku - front

Tora no Issoku - side

Ina Zuma - front

Ina Zuma - side

無雙直傳英信流居合術

Uki Gumo - front

Uki Gumo - side

Uki Gumo

This technique, performed with an opponent seated to our right, is the first introduction to *jujutsu* in the school. By *jujutsu*, I mean techniques and responses to attacks that are performed inside the attacking range of the sword (similar to *issoku ittō no maai* in kendo). Since we are practising a sword art, we must assume that our usual fighting range is that of the sword. When we get inside that sword range we must rely on special techniques, often involving specific body movements to deal with the situation.

This technique is of the *go no sen* variety, an avoidance of the attack and then a counterattack. After moving out of range of the grasping hand of the opponent, we draw (pushing a middle person out of the way) and cut into his shoulder from a very close distance by using a twist of the hips and a drop of the body with the hand held behind the plane of the hips. This lets us cut at a much shorter range than would normally be possible.

We then use an assisting hand on the back of the blade to help cut into the shoulder and drop the opponent to the ground where his arm or sleeve is trapped with the foot before the final cut from a "correct" distance.

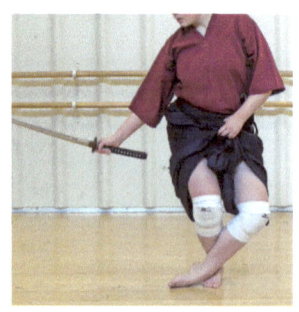

Yama Oroshi - front

Yama Oroshi - side

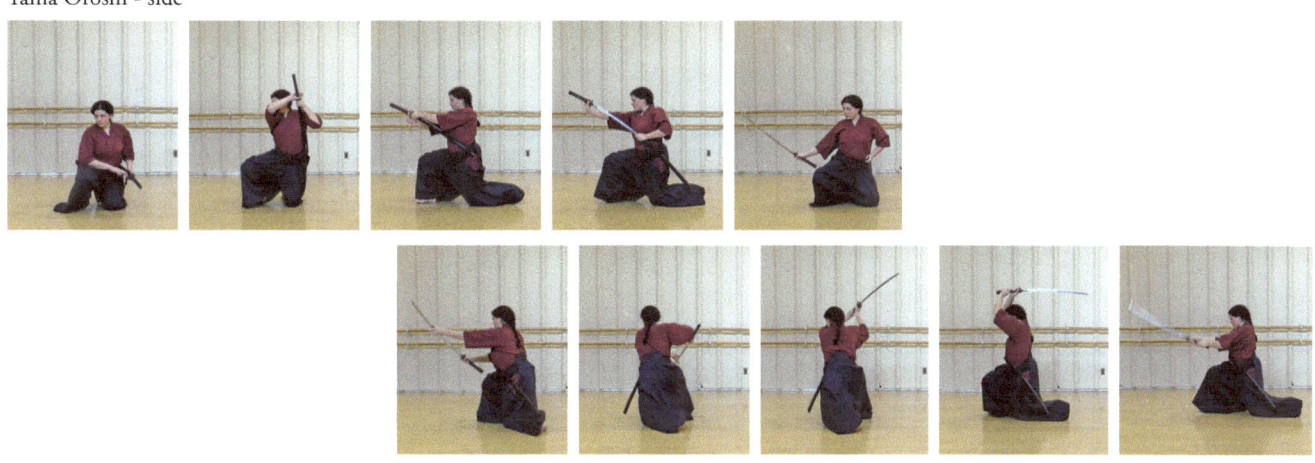

無雙直傳英信流居合術

With some imagination, one can develop a series of counterattacks from this sort of situation, and this has been done in some partner sets of practice in the art which are usually thought to be "lost". They are not lost, but have been preserved in some MSR lines. Be assured there is nothing shocking in these *kata*, they are simple and can be discovered with some willing students, a soft mat and a good knee brace to keep your left knee together.

Here is a simple variation: set up two fellow students to your right. The far student reaches in front of the person in the middle for your hilt. Just push the middle person into the far person to cause the opponent to fall over.

Oroshi

(Yama) Oroshi is performed with the opponent at an even closer distance. The timing is *sen sen no sen* (attack into the attack) as we move the *tsuka* to avoid the grab and in the same motion strike to the face with the *tsukagashira*. For even more jujutsu, as most people understand it, examine the various movements of the *tsuka* to escape a successful grab or to lock the wrist using the *tsuka* itself.

The cut into the chest is very close, and is done with the tip upward and hand behind the body once more. In some methods of practice, the knee or the hilt may be used to jam the opponent's hands as he tries to draw his own sword during this cut. The throwing down (using the sword) and final strike is done similar to Uki Gumo.

Iwa Nami - front

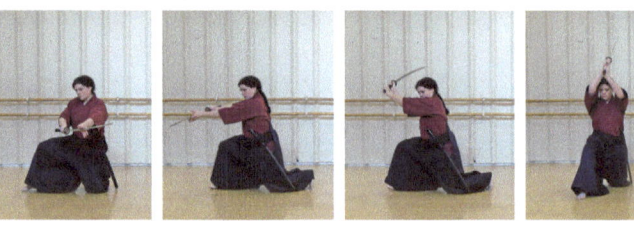

Iwa Nami - side

無雙直傳英信流居合術

Iwa Nami

This is the third of the Eishin-ryū "jujutsu" techniques and it is a *sen no sen* attack. These three *kata* show the three classic timings of combat (defend then attack, attacking at the same time, preemptive attack) along with close-quarter work using a sword.

This *kata* introduces the use of noise to provoke a reaction from the opponent, and to take advantage of his being surprised. The sword is drawn out of sight of the opponent, then as we line up the tip with his body we stamp to cause him to turn toward us. We then thrust into his torso, throw him to the right and cut down as per the previous *kata*.

The *kata* shows one way to deal with an opponent on the left who is very close; a dangerous situation as it is hard to draw and cut from this position. Again there is a shortening of the sword length by using the left hand on the back of the blade as we thrust into the opponent's abdomen. This *kata* is similar to numbers four and five but with the opponent in a new location. Surprisingly, this is also the first introduction or a thrust.

This set of three *kata* also has small variations. The opponent can be pulled down (*hiki-taoshi*) at 22, 45 and 90 degrees to the original attack line because this makes for subtle changes in the *maai*. As with the heights of the final cut and the movement forward or back, this can be saved until the student has enough body control to make the necessary changes. These formal changes in the *kata* are done in preparation for the final level of practice, the Oku Iai, which must be practised fluidly, as if reacting to changing attacks at all times.

Uroko Gaeshi - front

Uroko Gaeshi-side

Nami Gaeshi - front

Nami Gaeshi - side

Uroko Gaeshi

These next two *kata* revisit Ōmori-ryū as Migi and Ushiro are done from the starting *tatehiza* position.

Using *tatehiza* in Uroko Gaeshi enables both feet to be pulled back from the attack coming from the left side, rather than moving forward into it as is done in Migi. In this way the strike can be completely avoided and an opponent who is much closer can be dealt with better than in *seiza*. This is another way to deal with an opponent on our left hand side. We pull our toes up under ourselves (*kiza*) and turn to the left on them, then pull the left foot back, followed by the right, as we cut horizontally. The vertical cut is done as per Migi of Ōmori-ryū and we then finish with *yoko-chiburi* and *nōtō*.

If you wish to practise this *kata* with a partner using *bokutō*, have them initiate the attack from Oroshi to the side of your head with their hilt. You respond by moving both feet back and drawing in *nuki-tsuke* to cut their head, shoulder or right wrist as they complete their strike to where your head was. This will demonstrate nicely the movement from inside to correct *maai*.

Nami Gaeshi

Nami Gaeshi is Ushiro done from *tatehiza*. In this case, no shifting of the knee is necessary to deal with an opponent who is directly behind. Again both feet can be pulled back away from the attack so we have a much more useful response to the situation.

Try this *kata* using the same attack to the *saya* that was practised with a partner using Ushiro in the first set.

Taki Otoshi - front

Taki Otoshi - side

The Other Mae Kata

We do not do Hidari from *tatehiza*, but it is of course possible if so desired. A horizontal and then vertical cut from all the various directions are possible using these two *kata* (with Yoko Gumo representing Mae itself). This was the second set of "the same kata practised from different angles" that was mentioned in the Ōmori-ryū section.

Taki Otoshi

What if your opponent actually gets hold of your *saya* from behind and you cannot do Ushiro/Nami Gaeshi? This is the sort of question my self defence or aikido class would ask when returning to a jujutsu context.

In this *kata*, we release the *saya* by weakening that grip while standing upward and back, then stepping forward (away from the opponent) and pulling the *tsuka* upward, dropping the *kojiri* away from the grab. The opponent follows the *saya* in toward us (standing up) so that he is again inside the ideal sword range. Therefore, we place the sword largely behind ourselves, with the *mune* near the *kissaki* on our hip to deal with the close range and to ensure that the opponent does not simply slap the blade to the side. The thrust is changed from short to long range by extending the arm as the opponent retreats. He is chased in a similar movement to what is done in Yae Gaki in the Ōmori-ryū section. We drop down to our knee as we do a final vertical cut. It is here that the practitioner starts

Makko - front

Makko - side

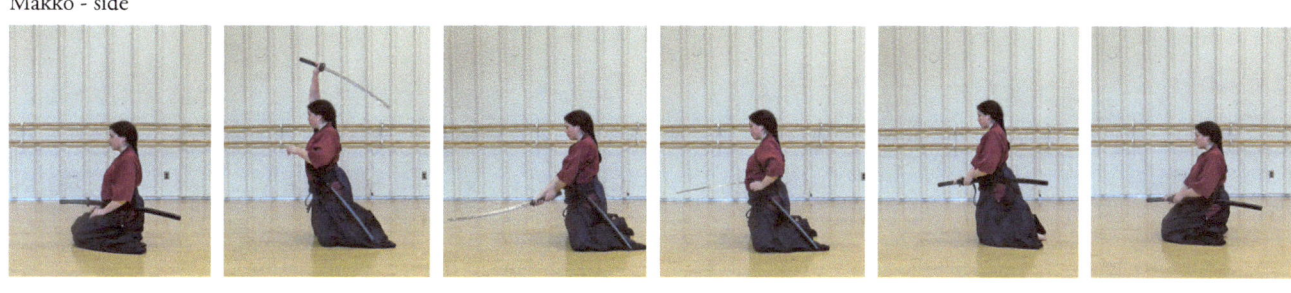

無雙直傳英信流居合術

to understand the difference between dropping while cutting and kneeling before cutting. This choice is made partly on what distance is available between practitioner and opponent.

Makko

This *kata* is done from *seiza* once more, and can be identical to Nuki Uchi in Ōmori-ryū, or it can be done in the more direct manner of *kiritsuke*—a cut downward from the draw rather than a draw then *furikaburi* and cut motion as is done in Ōmori. For those who practise AJKF *iai*, Nuki Uchi is done like the first movement of No.11 (Sō Giri) as an *ukenagashi*, and Makko is done like the draw and cut of No.12: directly overhead and down.

Final Notes on Eishin-ryū

In the Eishin-ryū, the practitioner is still dealing with single opponents, but has now been introduced to the benefits of *tatehiza* when seated. We have also been introduced to the *jūjutsu* of the school and this can be expanded if needed. With the two Ōmori-ryū and Eishin-ryū sets, practitioners should have received a thorough education in the basics and tactics of the school. These can be thought of as the alphabet, spelling and grammar. Now the practitioner is ready to begin writing whole sentences.

Uncle Kotay's Kendo Korner
Part 1: sonkyo in kendo

Q: Uncle Kotay, why do we have to do sonkyo in kendo? It's really awkward, not practical, and looks really bad when you lose balance at a grading. What's the point of it anyway? (#squatbot)

A: Everybody in Kendoland might be surprised to know that *sonkyo*, that odd squatting posture before the bout begins, has not been around that long in its current form. Something similar to *sonkyo* was introduced into some schools of swordsmanship around the middle of the Tokugawa period, sometime during the eighteenth century. This was about the same time the squatting ritual was introduced into sumo as well.

For example, the Jikishin Kage-ryū employed a movement called *kikyo* where swordsmen lowered their backsides and touched the ground with both hands before picking up their swords. As with sumo, this movement apparently enabled the swordsman to focus his energy in the lower abdomen, to control breathing, and lower his heartbeat. Apart from the physiological benefits, taking a lower posture was also considered a sign of respect, purity, and humility when entering a sacred space. Another term, *orishiki*, also referred to the motion of placing one knee on the ground before getting into it. Rather than for practical purposes, it was more a ceremonial sign of respect before starting the bout, and became widespread with the increase of inter-school matches and demonstrations, which were often performed in front of important people like a *daimyō*. Not all schools did this, and many preferred to start from the standing position.

The style of *sonkyo* that is performed in kendo today is a continuation of the *kikyo* and *orishiki* traditions, but was only introduced into the mainstream with the creation of the Nihon Kendo Kata in 1912. During the war years in Japan, *sonkyo* was actually done away with, and bouts started from the standing position. As Taiwan and Korea were under Japanese control until the end of the war, starting a kendo bout from the standing position has remained standard practice in those countries. FIK protocols, however, dictate that matches begin and end with *sonkyo*.

People with bad knees often have problems doing *sonkyo* properly. It is permissible to take the *orishiki* position instead—that is, kneeling with the left knee on the ground, and the right leg bent in front. Incidentally, kneeling in this way rather than squatting with both knees open was the standard method for women kenshi in the early years.

But I digress. What is the point? *Sonkyo* focuses *ki* in the lower abdomen, gets the mind and body in sync, is a sign of purity and respect where both kenshi start on an equal footing, and is a great way to build strength in the thighs and firm up those buttocks! *Sonkyo* pumpkins. It's gotta be good for you!

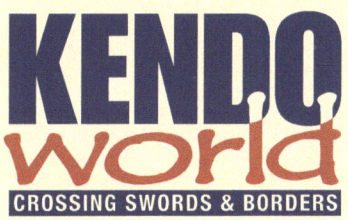

PUBLICATIONS
BACK ISSUES

The Kendo World Team is pleased to announce that all eight issues of Kendo World Volume 1 & 2, originally released between 2001 and 2004 and out of print for many years, are now available in Zinio digital format.

The good news doesn't end there though! We are working hard to also get volumes 3, 4, 5, and 6 ready so that our entire catalogue will be available on the Zinio platform!!

More info → www.kendo-world.com

A peek into the Tozando Iwate Factory
- Passing down the traditional arts of Bogu making

The Tozando Iwate Factory is located in Kuji in Iwate prefecture, Japan. Although it is not normally open to public, this time we have decided to provide an exclusive look into the Iwate factory and the production that goes on there.

Tozando is one of the few remaining large-scale Budo equipment makers in Japan that completes all of its work there. The Tozando Iwate Factory has over 30 skilled craftsmen, making everything from Aikido Gi and Hakama, to Kendo Bogu. Piece by piece, each product is painstakingly made by our craftsmen. We have some of the few remaining genuine craftsmen in Japan who create high quality 100% made in Japan Budo equipment for the domestic and international market.

Some of the popular products made in the Iwate Factory include our Mokkei Kote and Kendo Bogu, not to mention high quality Hakama and Gi uniforms that are favourites with many of our long-time customers.

Tozando has always stressed the importance of quality and tradition, and this is why we have put our utmost efforts in creating an optimal environment for passing down the traditional arts of Budo equipment production to the next generation. Tozando now has over 50 craftsmen working and producing Budo equipment in Kyoto and in our Iwate Factory.

The craftsmen in Tozando do not only stay true to tradition, but also embrace innovative ideas and techniques to create original products such as the Tozando Tornado-stitch and Custom-made Kote. This is unique to Tozando, as no other company can offer the same level of customization.

This is all made possible by the master craftsmen at Tozando with their long experience and eagerness to keep honing their skills, inheriting the true spirit of Japanese craftsmanship.

Please experience true quality for yourself!

Tozando Co.,Ltd.
www.tozando.com

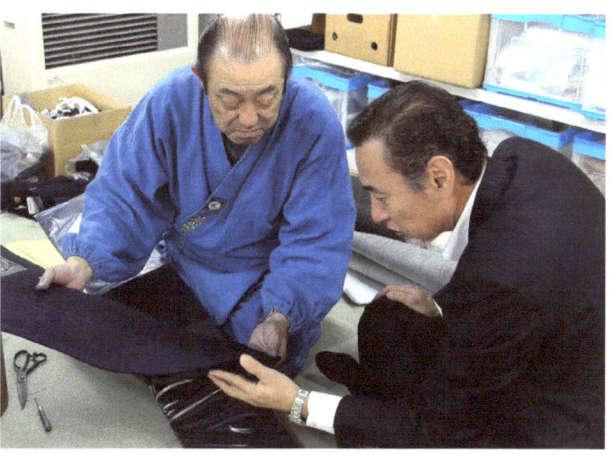

President of Tozando, Mr. Kimura Takahiko and Master Bogu Craftsman, Mr. Nagasaki Tatsuo, inspecting the quality of a Men Futon

To everyone who loves Kendo
— A message from the Tozando Iwate Factory!

In the current Japanese Bogu industry, many makers have resorted to producing their Bogu overseas to reduce costs in an increasingly competitive market. Lamentably, lower quality Bogu available on the market today has become the industry standard. Making Bogu increasingly flexible and light to promote usability while keeping the costs down has resulted in equipment that has lost its true function—to protect the user from harm.

We at Tozando swear to continue to pursue quality and durability that can only be produced in Japan. While our skills are firmly based on traditional Bogu making techniques, we also stay open to new ideas and innovative methods to produce products unique to Tozando. We will continue to make Bogu in Japan that are true to the meaning of "Bogu", which is the pride of all craftsmen who work at Tozando.

We hope that our hard work and efforts can bring you joy while practicing Budo!

Nagasaki Tatsuo
Master Bogu Craftsman

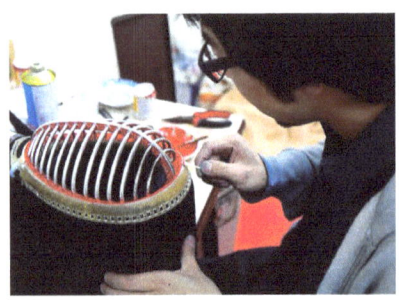

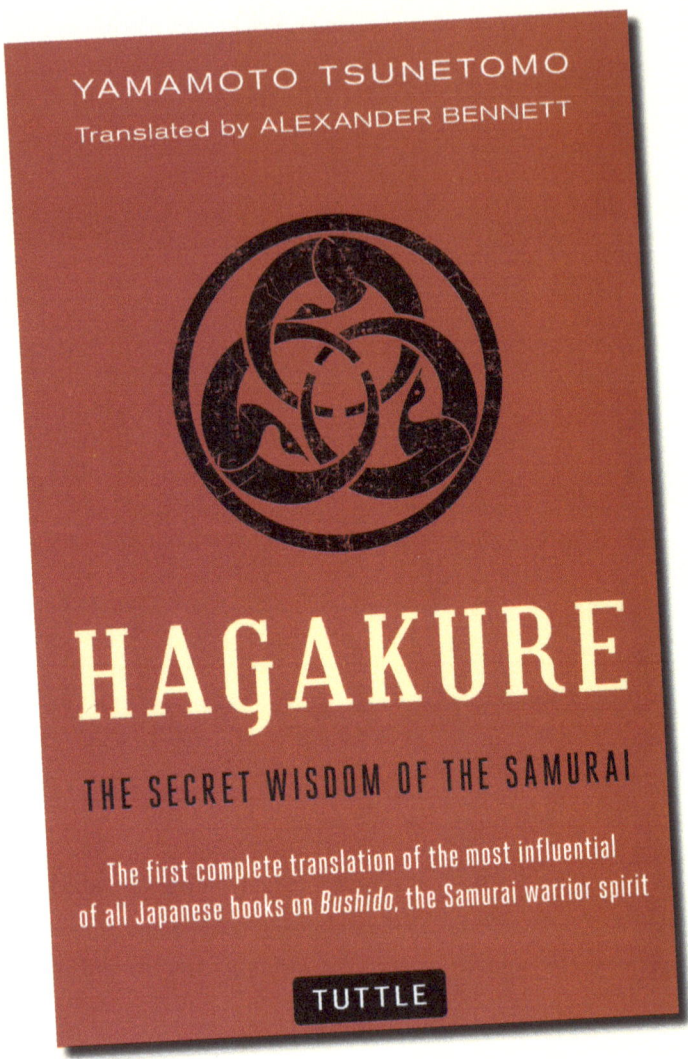

"Alex Bennett has produced the first truly authoritative translation and analysis of Hagakure—*perhaps the most famous text ever written about samurai honor*—to appear in any Western language. Simultaneously erudite and accessible, this volume belongs on the bookshelves of anyone—scholar or hobbyist alike—interested in samurai culture, or modern perceptions thereof."

— Dr. Karl F. Friday, author of *Samurai, Warfare and the State in Early Medieval Japan* and *Japan Emerging: Premodern History to 1850*

"[Alex Bennett] is the very best writer on martial arts alive today and [his] work needs to be showcased to the general public."

— Don Warrener, President, *Budo International*

"Dr. Bennett possesses a profound knowledge of, and deep insight into, the world of Japanese bushido. This expertise has been enhanced by his extensive practical experience of the traditional martial arts of Japan, and his proficiency in this domain is highly acclaimed."

— Tetsuo Yamaori, former Director of the International Research Center for Japanese Studies

"[A] strong point is a scholarly and succinct introduction that grounds the work in historical and social context, equipping the reader with a cultural map of Yamamoto's world. Footnotes provide valuable background and add resonance throughout, keeping names and familial relations straight, highlighting pertinent cross-references and generally rendering the work accessible to contemporary readers."

— *The Japan Times*

Search for "Bennett" and "Hagakure" on Amazon.com